Social Causation and Biographical Research

This book extends debates in the field of biographical research, arguing that causal explanations are not at odds with biographical research and that biographical research is in fact a valuable tool for explaining why things in social and personal lives are one way and not another. Bringing reconstructive biographical research into dialogue with critical realism, it explains how and why relational social ontology can become a unique theoretical ground for tapping emergent mechanisms and latent meaning structures. Through an account of the reasons for which reductionist epistemologies, rational action models and covering law explanations are not appropriate for biographical research, the authors develop the philosophical idea of singular causation as a means by which biographical researchers are able to forge causal hypotheses for the occurrence of events and offer guidance on the application of this methodological principle to concrete, empirical examples. As such, this volume will appeal to scholars across the social sciences with interests in biographical research and social research methods.

Giorgos Tsiolis is Associate Professor of Qualitative Methods in Sociological Research and currently Head of the Department of Sociology at the University of Crete, Greece.

Michalis Christodoulou teaches in the Department of Philosophy at the University of Patras, Greece. He is the co-editor of *Emotions, Temporalities and Working-Class Identities in the 21st Century*.

Routledge Advances in Research Methods

Defending Qualitative Research
Design, Analysis and Textualization
Mario Cardano

Researching Ageing
Methodological Challenges and their Empirical Background
Edited by Maria Łuszczyńska

Diagramming the Social
Relational Method in Research
Russell Dudley-Smith and Natasha Whiteman

Participatory Case Study Work
Approaches, Authenticity and Application in Ageing Studies
Edited by Sion Williams and John Keady

Social Causation and Biographical Research
Philosophical, Theoretical and Methodological Arguments
Georgios Tsiolis and Michalis Christodoulou

Beyond Disciplinarity
Historical Evolutions of Research Epistemology
Catherine Hayes, John Fulton and Andrew Livingstone with Claire Todd, Stephen Capper and Peter Smith

For more information about this series, please visit: www.routledge.com/Routledge-Advances-in-Research-Methods/book-series/RARM

Social Causation and Biographical Research

Philosophical, Theoretical and Methodological Arguments

Giorgos Tsiolis and Michalis Christodoulou

Routledge
Taylor & Francis Group

LONDON AND NEW YORK

First published 2021
by Routledge
2 Park Square, Milton Park, Abingdon, Oxon OX14 4RN

and by Routledge
605 Third Avenue, New York, NY 10017

First issued in paperback 2022

Routledge is an imprint of the Taylor & Francis Group, an informa business

British Library Cataloguing-in-Publication Data
A catalogue record for this book is available from the British Library

Library of Congress Cataloging-in-Publication Data
Names: Tsiolis, Giorgos, 1967- author. | Christodoulou, Michalēs, author.
Title: Social causation and biographical research: philosophical, theoretical and methodological arguments / Georgios Tsiolis and Michalis Christodoulou.
Description: Milton Park, Abingdon, Oxon; New York, NY: Routledge, 2021. | Includes bibliographical references and index.
Identifiers: LCCN 2020028491 (print) | LCCN 2020028492 (ebook) | ISBN 9780367620363 (hardback) | ISBN 9781003107613 (ebook)
Subjects: LCSH: Social sciences--Biographical methods.
Classification: LCC HD61.29 .T75 2021 (print) | LCC HD61.29 (ebook) | DDC 300.72/2--dc23
LC record available at https://lccn.loc.gov/2020028491
LC ebook record available at https://lccn.loc.gov/2020028492

ISBN: 978-0-367-62039-4 (pbk)
ISBN: 978-0-367-62036-3 (hbk)
ISBN: 978-1-003-10761-3 (ebk)

DOI: 10.4324/9781003107613

Typeset in Times New Roman
by Deanta Global Publishing Services, Chennai, India

Contents

Figures

Abbreviations

CR	Critical realism
D-N	Deductive-nomological
LMS	Latent meaning structures
OH	Objective hermeneutic
RBR	Reconstructive biographical research

1   Introduction

Singular causation and biographical research

In the social sciences, there are three ways through which social researchers can claim explanatory theories: the deductive-nomological (D-N) model, empathy and generative mechanisms. Roughly speaking, these have their philosophical foundations in positivism, hermeneutics–interpretivism and critical realism (CR), respectively. In the first case, I know something only if I know the general law in which it is subsumed; in the second case, I know something only if I can make it intelligible by specifying an agent's beliefs and desires; and in the third case, I know something only if I know what made it what it is. In the past, the deductive-nomological model of explanation enjoyed a monopoly over the meaning of the term "explanation", while hermeneutics was the major opponent to such a crude and positivistic account. However, in the last twenty years, mechanism-based explanations have come to constitute a third, distinct philosophical approach to social causation, providing more subtle and promising ideas than the other two, even though some of its assumptions have been shaped by the former. Nevertheless, as we demonstrate in the rest of the book, the proponents of causal mechanisms have tried to differentiate themselves both from the D-N approach and from the statistical Hume-inspired view of causation.

Needless to say, this development has a long history in the philosophy of science, but it has only been in recent years that social scientists have endeavoured to implement most of these philosophical ideas in the realm of social theory and methodology. In this sense, our book is not a treatise on the philosophy of science, but rather aims to elucidate how socio-ontological and epistemological ideas from the philosophy of social science may provide a new language for approaching causal analysis in the philosophy and methodology of qualitative social research. The bedrock of this new language is "causal explanation" and the reason is that a paradigm shift has taken place in the philosophy of social science. This shift has to do with social scientists gradually acknowledging the need for explaining social phenomena causally, rather than just describing them thickly. We believe that systematic dialogue between the philosophy of social science and social research would be very fruitful for the simple reason that philosophers provide answers regarding, for example, in what sense a social entity is social, while social scientists investigate empirically the extent to which these answers are viable in research practice. In a similar vein, Joas and Knöbl (2009, 16) dispute the division of labour between those who

> see themselves as theoreticians and those who view themselves as empiricists or empirical social researchers. These two groupings scarcely register each other's findings any more. But theoretical and empirical knowledge cannot truly be separated. This lecture on the "nature" of theory is thus intended to provide us with an opportunity to think about what theory is, its importance to empirical research and the way in which empirical knowledge always informs its theoretical counterpart.

This book defends the view that a science of society is possible by taking into account a limited naturalism through which quantitative and qualitative research approaches participate in a mutually profitable dialogue. This can be achieved, we believe, not by taking physics or physicalism as a model but by showing how causal thinking can be inserted into the ontological and epistemological assumptions through which social scientists make sense of the entities of the social world. Although a great many scholars have presented various arguments as to how causal thinking may sustain quantitative methods, we believe that causal thinking has not yet been implemented in the social ontologies and epistemologies of the qualitative tradition. The reason is well known and has to do with the main interpretivist ontological thesis that the social is meaningful. Without disputing the merits of such a thesis, we believe that it cannot constitute the ground for social policy measures exactly because it prioritizes thick descriptions and not causal explanations. Without causal knowledge of why things happen or why social processes are of this nature and not another, policy interventions are mere guesses in the dark.

According to Kincaid (1996), the adoption of naturalism as a social ontology for qualitative research has been attacked from two angles. First, from those who believe that causality is a law-like conception of approaching social action that is not only inappropriate but also dangerous for social sciences because humans are depicted as not being active agents. What qualitative researchers should do is grasp the meaning of social action through empathy. In this way, the goal of objectivity is but a dream, because even scientists see things from their own point of view. A more radical denial of accepting naturalism in qualitative social science comes from Kuhn-inspired arguments that see social science as a form of rhetoric or as a social institution in which knowledge is a product of power relations or social conventions. Second, there are those who have been identified with positivist thinking, where what counts as scientific is only whatever is measurable and can be verified through the methods of physics. Those who adopt these views talk about causality and unification based on the ideal of how physicists practise science.

In contrast to both of these views, we believe that social science can claim causal knowledge of the social world by making use of non-experimental evidence and of evidence related to "texts" (interviews, field notes) and not only to "numbers". This is a difficult project because we have to be very clear about how we conceive of causality, given that this is a plural term with more than one possible approach available (Reiss 2009). In addition, we have to show in detail in what sense a knowledge of the social connected with qualitative methods can be causal and how a mechanism-based account of causality can be of use for qualitative researchers. Within the relevant literature three issues seem to be the most controversial. The first concerns whether findings of causal mechanisms are transferable and generalizable or not (Knight 2009); the second concerns whether theoretical understandings concerning mechanisms are formal or substantive (Gross 2009) and the third concerns where they have to be searched: on the individual and the action level, or on the emergent level of social groups, social relations, structures and institutions (Sawyer 2004).

At the beginning of this book, we have to state clearly some of the philosophical ideas pertaining to a well-known (and for some, highly disputed) distinction between two kinds of properties: the primary properties of the physical world, which are mind-independent; and the phenomenal properties or qualia, which depend on the subject. In Kantian terminology, the first kinds of non-phenomenal properties, referring to things-in-themselves, are called "noumena"; while the second kinds of properties, referring to things-as-perceived, are called "phenomena". The philosophical tradition of phenomenalism has determined the genesis of qualitative research. As Bunge (2006) has noted, this tradition holds a specific stance regarding qualia, namely that only phenomena exist in the sense that existence depends on perception, so whatever is beyond phenomenalists' ken (primary properties related to the world) is regarded as either unknowable or inexistent. For phenomenalists, only phenomena or qualia can be known. This kind of ontological and epistemological phenomenalism is the background assumption of both the reductionist aspirations of ontological individualists discussed in the second chapter and of Verstehen social theorists. Both of these currents tend to exaggerate the importance of individual motives and decisions at the expense of holistic realities like social structures or social relations, the properties of which reside in the outer social reality. By assuming that without sentient beings there is no universe, phenomenalists (and qualitative researchers) prefer to retreat from reality or to remain indifferent to explaining social transformations. In contrast to the epistemology and ontology of phenomenalism, in this book we hold the thesis that qualia are not exclusively psychological occurrences or mental states but rather are relational properties. Although qualia are first-person processes that do not exist in the physical world, they emerge from the encounter of the subject and the world. Only on condition of a relational social ontology can causal explanations be claimed as third-person observations that identify why things occur in specific ways. In short, no third-person perspective, no scientific advancement. The corollary for social science may be that people's perceptions of the external world (that is, qualia) can be studied as "noumena" and that appearances call for explanation in terms of unobservable relational properties, instead of being explainers. This is why the third chapter is devoted to elaborating the premises of this social ontology.

Traditionally, the most used approach to causal explanations in social science stems from individual-oriented ontological premises that state that a mechanism-based explanation should analyze the details of the rationality of individual action. Remaining faithful to the abovementioned phenomenalist philosophical dogma, ontological individualists hold that social mechanisms are found on the level of individual action and are liable to being modelled by scientists in order to predict similar actions. One other feature of this kind of approach to social mechanisms is its emphasis on theorizing the substantive level of causality and on identifying how it works within specific domains of reality. Gundersen (2018) maintains that a mechanism-based explanation grounded on ontological individualism is a threat to the autonomy of the social sciences because of the reductionism it entails, as the emergent upper-level strata can be explained by reference to their lower and elementary particulars. Although this belief sounds logical, we do not think that this threat should make us dismissive of humans' reasoning. For us, a working definition of a mechanism is that a mechanism-based explanation claims that to explain a phenomenon, one must consider how it is generated through the interactions among its constituents. As a consequence, we think that social science can successfully explain processes of the social world without copying the premises of the D-N model and without being afraid of adopting a realist view towards mental entities.

We hold that the main problem with ontological individualism is its reliance on rational action theory and its inability to explain real-life experiences. For this reason, in this book we focus on what the idea of social emergentism has to confer on the issue of explanation because of two ideas that we deem crucial for the philosophical and methodological grounding of social research: the first is the concept of non-reductive relational properties and the second is that by studying the particular/singular, one can gain knowledge of the universal. Both of these ideas rest on the thesis that knowing the social world is to think causally about it and that even if human actions are meaningful, they can still be causally explained. It is on this thesis that the first four chapters of the book are focused. We believe that this thesis is what differentiates the contemporary version of methodological holism from its traditional expression in social theory, structuralism and functionalism. Instead of reproducing well-known interpretivists' dictates, like that of prioritizing the meaningfulness of the social or of critiquing power relations, we aim to explore the (ontological and epistemological) conditions under which qualitative research (especially reconstructive biographical research, RBR) can claim causal explanations of the social world and detect generative mechanisms that make things happen.

Mechanism-based accounts of causality are usually grouped under three theoretical traditions. First is the pragmatist conception of causality, in which causal explanations in social science prioritize social action as a problem-solving activity (Gross 2009). Despite its impact on qualitative research and its profound contribution of the methodological insights of "abduction", we think that the pragmatist approach to mechanism-based accounts of causality remains committed to a flat social ontology that fails to take into account how and why specific social situations become problematic for social actors. Given that this is a huge and disputable statement that deserves deep analysis, we do not deal with this issue in our book. The second approach sees causality as a process-tracing procedure that tries to identify the path leading from one event (the cause) to another (the effect) and to describe these intermediary steps (Mahoney 2008; Ragin 2008). The causality-as-process-tracing approach states that what researchers need to do is to describe the details of the path connecting two distinct events. Although promising and enabling causal explanations for qualitative research, it is more focused on the methodological particularities of causality, not on the theoretical and epistemological grounding for explaining emergent phenomena. The third approach to mechanisms is inscribed within the CR tradition which is thoroughly presented in the third chapter.

We must stress that "mechanism" is a causal notion in the sense that it describes the entities that make something happen or that produce something, informing us about how entities, their relations and their properties give rise to the phenomenon of interest. It has been argued that the definition of mechanism propounded by the philosophers Machamer, Darden and Craver (2000: 3) is the one that fits best with the entities treated by the biological and social sciences. These authors say that "mechanisms are entities and activities organized such that they are productive of regular changes from start or set-up to finish or termination conditions". More refined versions of this definition are that "a mechanism for a phenomenon consists of entities and activities organized in such a way that they are responsible for the phenomenon" (Illari and Williamson 2012, 121) and that "a mechanism for a phenomenon consists of entities (or parts) whose activities and interactions are organized in such a way that they produce the phenomenon" (Glennan 2017, 14). One crucial component of these definitions is that they dispute the Humean and regularity conception of causality in so far as mechanisms can work only once or irregularly. The relevance of a mechanism-based explanation is that it identifies the difference that entities, properties and their interactions make to the outcomes of interest. If the presence of an entity or of changes in its properties or activities truly does not make any difference to the effect to be explained, it can be ignored.

The approach to causation upon which we try to articulate our argument for framing causality through biographical research accepts two things about causality. First, the term "causality" is not equivalent to determinism, designating a causal connection between states of affairs, outcomes or events. Second, we see causality primarily as an ontological term in the sense that causal connections are a trait of the things themselves, not solely a way of knowing things. We hold that logical necessities are quite different from social necessities because a logical connection is not always causal given that it does not produce something. In other words, Humean constant conjunctions between events A and B are not causal because they are logically necessary, but only on the condition that they exhibit traits of the world by means of which A makes B what it is and not something else. Instead of prioritizing that things in social life happen by chance, we defend the idea that causal conditions exist that may affect how things happen in a specified manner. This is synonymous neither with exceptionless regularities nor with prediction and the reason is that social facts are imbued with openness; they are not closed systems susceptible to prediction. As Bunge (2009) has noted, the most important feature of causality is its productive character in the sense that something gives rise to something else, as nothing can arise out of nothing.

In addition, in this book we are committed to the idea that there is no privileged theory of causation that applies to all sciences, from the basic ones (physics, chemistry) to the special ones (biological and social sciences). For instance, in some of the social sciences like sociology or economics, the interventionist theory of causation cannot easily be sustained. This theory states that X is a cause of Y if and only if there is a possible intervention in X that changes Y. An intervention is a manipulation of the cause – and only of the cause – that is supposed, in principle, to be possible. Regression models for predicting the values of the dependent variable are those most used by social scientists. However, the linear assumptions connected with this model have been repeatedly criticized by Andrew Abbott (2007) because social life has a processual and stratified nature, the complexity of which cannot be understood through them. The notion of process-oriented causation proposed by Abbott is in line with actual causation, which is related to token events, as opposed to type-level causation, which is related to event-types. The latter says that "type-C events cause type-E events", while claims about actual causation are of the form "the event-token c causes the event-token e" (Reutlinger 2013, 15). Be that as it may, social scientists converge on the following criteria for considering a causal claim adequate: modal relation (causes enforce and produce their effects); time-asymmetry of causation (causes precede their effects in time, not vice versa); causal asymmetry (the causal relation is asymmetric; that is, if X causes Y, then Y does not cause X); distinction of spurious correlation and genuine causation (the correlation is obtained due to a common cause Z); and context (X causes Y because of the peculiarity of the context).

We consider these criteria as constituting a general framework of causation which could be used by qualitative social scientists for approaching social phenomena. For that reason, it is not by accident that that singular causation can become a philosophical background for carrying out biographical research, because this manner of conceiving causal relations states that singular causal relations can exist even if there are no causal laws that connect types of events of which these causes and effects are instances. According to this conception, singular causal relations are not instantiations of some wider law and, in this sense, they are not reduced to the law. The singular is not reduced to the general in conformity with a nominalist social ontology. However, how can singular causation be of use in biographical research? If causal laws need not be present for causal relations to take place, then how does one explain people's biographical trajectories? Does it mean that the causes are to be identified in their reasons for action and in their intentions? We propose the idea that the answer must be sought, not in people's reasons for action, but in the properties of the social relations within which people live over the course of their lives. This answer necessitates a social ontology quite different from that which prioritizes the idea that people are rational actors who pursue goals. In contrast to these intentional explanations of action, we believe that biographies can be explained only on condition that one conceives of humans as beings that are in relation with others. This kind of relational social ontology holds that the properties of the relation are not reduced to the properties of its parts, without this meaning that the relations are wholes with a discrete essence. One of the main contributions of this book is that CR provides a framework for identifying causality at the emergent level of relations through its conceptualization of "mechanisms".

"Relational mechanisms" is a distinctive term propounded by critical realists through which one can explain the singular not by reducing it to agents' reasons for actions or to pre-defined social structures, but to the peculiarities of the forms of the social relations they experience in various periods of their lives. Note here that by studying biographies, one is not limited to studying disconnected singulars. Biographies are instances of the traces left by generative mechanisms connected to specific cases of wider phenomena. In this sense, the merit of studying biographies is not only to give voice to particular social groups regarding how their members experience the social world, but to explain why a specific state of affairs went in that direction and not another, or why it took that form and not another.

In this book we put in motion the relational paradigm of social ontology according to the version put forward by CR. Given that there are various socio-theoretical traditions conceptualizing the relational nature of the social, we think that the critical realist version is the most appropriate for grounding biographical research. The following are some of several reasons for this choice. First, because γνῶθι σ' εαυτόν (self-knowledge) is tied up with knowing what it means for a human to be related to others. By studying social relations, one has access both to how individuals reason about their everyday lives and to how society is transformed. Second, because agents' reasons for action are not devalued as "spontaneous sociologies" but are seriously taken into account so that causal explanations can be obtained. Third, because the conception of humans put forward by the relational paradigm, rather than mimicking the rational actor pursuing the maximization of goals, theorizes agency in a non-voluntaristic way and without bringing the "internalization of the exteriority" in through the back door. The main idea of a relational epistemology is that humans, in being with others, create social forms that can be human or non-human. The social is human when actors are reciprocally oriented and create such social objects as families, states or hospitals and monuments. The relationality of these forms makes them present emergent properties that are irreducible to each individual. Emergence denotes that the social is composed of layers that should not be understood in an aggregative way; on the contrary, each level presents properties, the nature of which depends on the configuration of its parts; these are novel in comparison to the lower level. The newness of these emergent properties also entails new causal powers that affect lower-level properties. We will say more on this issue in chapters 2 and 3, but at the moment one has to bear in mind that the emergent properties of people's social forms are a promising idea for claiming causal explanations through biographical research.

A relevant issue concerns how causal explanations in biographical research can be generalizable. In this book we argue that generalizability depends on case selection and on how relational mechanisms are connected with contexts across cases. The identification of relational mechanisms is not deduced from social laws or from regularities; rather, one should proceed in a retroductive way from the case to the phenomenon. In the fifth chapter we elaborate on this idea and in particular we show how by identifying through RBR the relational nature of the causal chain giving rise to a state of affairs, one can sharpen his/her concepts for explaining the phenomenon of interest.

Outline of the book

Our book aims to deal with these intriguing issues and provide a unifying philosophical, theoretical and methodological framework through which social phenomena can be seen in causal terms. Causal mechanisms are the central concept of this enterprise. However, in stating this, one is not saying much about how one can explain what makes things happen. This is why we have decided to forge an argument that will refer not only to the methodological details for achieving causality but also to the philosophical and theoretical grounds regarding how a mechanism-based explanation can be of use to biographical researchers. In the following paragraphs we will clarify how we have organized this argumentation in the chapters of the book.

In *chapter 2*, we summarize the main philosophical arguments which state that a mechanism-based explanation can be implemented only on the condition that one subscribes to a reductive epistemological line of reasoning. We provide details of the reasons why reductionism is doomed to fail and why it cannot constitute the ground for qualitative research, much less for biographical research. In addition, we show how one can combine a mechanism-based explanation with biographical research not by resorting to reductionism, but to singular causality and to the process-tracing conception of causality. We believe that CR is an appropriate philosophical framework with which these two conceptions of causality are coherent.

Chapter 3 presents details of how CR makes sense of social causation. We describe the affinities between Bhaskar's three-level ontology and Donati's theory of relational mechanisms. One of the main ideas that we believe CR offers to biographical research concerns how forms of social relations present emergent properties that affect people's lived experiences causally.

In *chapter 4*, we analyze three crucial theoretical steps needed for one to achieve causality through biographical research. First, the concept of "casing" is the *par excellence* means of identifying causal hypotheses which shed light on the conditions that make things happen in a specific way and not another. Second, by using social science examples drawn from qualitative research, we show how Mackie's INUS condition can provide researchers with tools for delineating the scope of their causal arguments. Finally, we illustrate how Ragin's set-theoretic conception of constructing cases provides a powerful means for theory development.

In *chapter 5*, we discuss in detail the arguments developed by various scholars on the relation of the singular to the general or how explanatory accounts drawn from qualitative research may be transferred to contexts other than those in which they were produced. We illustrate through specific examples of biographical research the relevance of typological theorizing and of causal chains for generalizing via mechanisms.

Chapters 6, 7 and *8* analyze how a specific strand of biographical research – RBR – may be implemented through the concept of relational mechanism as a frame for causal explanation.

In particular, in *chapter 6* we show why the interconnectedness between Archer's relational subject and Oevermann's latent meaning structures (LMS) is the intersection point through which the relational, processual and transformative character of "lived experience" is highlighted. We explore in depth how a surplus of meanings that developed into social relations come to be formed through subjects' practical involvement with the world. A pre-reflective knowing of the world is viewed as a precondition for habitual actions as well as for reflexive thinking.

Chapter 7 delineates the sense in which the temporal structuring of biographies is the key to uncovering causation regarding how agents take decisions. In particular, we show how the temporal grounding of self-formation enables researchers carrying out RBR to trace the morphostatic and morphogenetic relational mechanisms of various social phenomena. In addition, we provide detailed answers to the objections raised by radical social constructivists regarding the ontological reference of biographical interviews.

In *chapter 8* we provide a comprehensive account as to how Gabriele Rosenthal's principles of case reconstruction can shed light on causal connections. We elaborate on the interplay that exists between RBR's tripartite scheme of LMS, narrated life and experiencing life history and CR's three-level analysis of experiences, events and mechanisms. Finally, we show how relational mechanisms give shape to latent meaning structures and to the possibility of transforming them due to the contingency that frames them.

At the end, in the *epilogue* we summarize the main ideas of the argumentation of the whole book.

References

Abbott, A. "Mechanisms and Relations." *Sociologica* 2 (2007): 1–22. doi:10.2383/24750.

Bunge, M. *Chasing Reality: Strife Over Realism.* Toronto: University of Toronto Press, 2006.

Bunge, M. *Causality and Modern Science.* New York: Dover Publications, 2009.

Glennan, S. *The New Mechanical Philosophy.* Oxford: Oxford University Press, 2017.

Gross, N. "A Pragmatist Theory of Social Mechanisms." *American Sociological Review* 74, no. 3 (2009): 358–79. doi:10.1177/000312240907400302.

Gundersen, S. "Mechanism-Based Explanations Versus Autonomy in the Social Sciences." *Sociological Bulletin* 67, no. 1 (2018): 1–16. doi:10.1177/0038022917751976.

Illari, P.M., and J. Williamson. "What Is a Mechanism? Thinking About Mechanisms Across the Sciences." *European Journal for the Philosophy of Science* 2, no. 1 (2012): 119–35. doi:10.1007/s13194-011-0038-2.

Joas, H., and W. Knöbl. *Social Theory. Twenty Introductory Lectures.* Cambridge: Cambridge University Press, 2009.

Kincaid, H. *Philosophical Foundations of the Social Sciences. Analyzing Controversies on Social Research.* Cambridge: Cambridge University Press, 1996.

Knight, J. "Comment: Causal Mechanisms and Generalizations." In *Philosophy of the Social Sciences. Philosophical Theory and Scientific Practice*, edited by C. Mantzavinos, 179–85. Cambridge: Cambridge University Press, 2009.

Machamer, P., L. Darden, and C.F. Craver. "Thinking About Mechanisms." *Philosophy of Science* 67, no. 1 (2000): 1–25. doi:10.1086/392759.

Mahoney, J. "Toward a Unified Theory of Causality." *Comparative Political Studies* 41, no. 4–5 (2008): 412–36. doi:10.1177/0010414007313115.

Ragin, C.C. *Redesigning Social Inquiry. Fuzzy Sets and Beyond.* Chicago and London: University of Chicago Press, 2008.

Reiss, J. "Causation in the Social Sciences. Evidence, Inference and Purpose." *Philosophy of the Social Sciences* 39, no. 1 (2009): 20–40. doi:10.1177/0048393108328150.

Reutlinger, A. *A Theory of Causation in the Social and Biological Sciences.* New York: Palgrave Macmillan, 2013.

Sawyer, R.K. "The Mechanisms of Emergence." *Philosophy of the Social Sciences* 34, no. 2 (2004): 260–85. doi:10.1177/0048393103262553.

2 Philosophical arguments on social causality

Cases of reductionism

Although philosophical literature on causal explanation is vast and sometimes seems chaotic, social scientists have adopted many of these ideas in order to frame causality in all kinds of social research, both quantitative and qualitative. A common theme permeating these ideas is that the deductive-nomological model of Hempel presents too many inadequacies and shortcomings to be considered as a gold standard for social science research, especially for the qualitative approach. The main reasons are twofold: first, to the extent that the explanandum (that which is to be explained, for example a consumptive practice or a political attitude) is subsumed under the initial conditions of the explananda (that which explains, for example, a theoretical proposition covering all the particulars to which it refers), it follows that the particular finding is explained by reference to the premises of the initial conditions. For economists, these premises are identified via rational action theory, which aims to unify all the explanatory propositions of economic and social phenomena. However, in this sense – and this is the second reason behind the failure of the deductive-nomological (D-N) model – these kinds of social explanations are not informative about the social world. Indeed, they do not tell us something new in relation to the findings we have at our disposal after the research is finished. For the D-N model, whatever is not subsumed under the initial conditions of explananda is inexplicable and hence lacks the necessary armour for theory development (Keat and Urry 1975).

Mechanism-based causal explanations have been proposed as one way of overcoming the deficiencies stemming from the D-N model. This solution is premised on two ideas: first that what exists is only the particulars or the individuals (ontological individualism); and second that the explanation of social phenomena can be reduced to these particular individual-level details (methodological individualism). This demand for micro-foundations – as far as the explanation of social facts is concerned – has taken various forms. As Epstein (2014) has argued, many theorists endorse methodological individualism, while many others deny it in the sense that there are some ontological individualists who are trying to theorize when and under what conditions social wholes can have specific attributes or can be attributed mental states. However, what unites all of them is the denial of attributing explanatory (or causal) value to the properties of the whole. This means that although the concept of explanation is epistemological, we will present the varieties of methodological individualists in relation to how they conceive of social wholes, because it is their ontological commitments that explain their appeal to micro-foundations or to atomistic-laden conceptions of mechanisms.

Mechanism-based explanations in the social sciences, more or less, have been identified with weaker versions of methodological individualism, for which mechanisms are related to humans' reasoning; they do not belong to the furniture of the social world, as we will try to show in the next chapter. Micro-foundations refer to causal micro-linkages (Coleman 1994; Little 2012) that show in what ways a macro phenomenon is happening. In this sense, mechanism-based explanations are reductive explanations to the extent that only the micro-level events of the explanation constitute the mechanism of the phenomenon of interest. In trying to deal with this reductionist image, Ylikoski (2012) maintains that there are four ways through which one can conceive of the reality of macro social properties. His idea is that, first, one should not view micro-macro relations in categorical terms but as a continuum, in which how one conceives of the micro-level is a matter of degree. He makes the case that the macro properties of macro social entities like populations can be distributions and frequencies. When social scientists describe, for example, differences regarding the life plans of medical and philology students, they are interested in explaining variations between frequencies that are not dependent on members' beliefs and attitudes about them. The members of the population can have false, or even crazy, beliefs about distributions and frequencies that characterize their own society. Besides populations, second, macro social entities can be seen as irreducible to individuals if one views them as social networks. The ties between the members of a specified population present such characteristics as centralization, cohesion, density or structural cohesion, which are not reducible to individual persons. Third, another way of talking about the irreducibility of the social is the case of culture, customs and social norms in which the properties of the communities' members are shared. Fourth, organizations are more demarcated than cultural groups because they have prescribed rights and duties, stability, continuity and specified criteria for membership.

However, for Ylikoski, these four cases should not be conceived of as having an autonomous level of reality; they describe more extensive facts than the descriptions of the individual attitudes, habits, and preferences that constitute them and do not downwardly and causally influence lower levels of reality. Everything happens at the same level. This way of viewing society is ontologically flat, because the difference between micro and macro is one of scale, not of different levels. For Ylikoski (2013), this idea is grounded on the distinction between causation and constitution. Causation is about the relation between two distinct events, of which one is the cause of the other and which are connected through causal processes. By manipulating the cause, the effect is manipulated, too. By contrast, constitution is about the relation between properties: the properties of the parts are the properties of the system. In constitution, the whole is made of its parts and their relations and hence the parts can exist independently of the whole but not the other way round. While a causal explanation tells us how the antecedent events and their organization bring about the event to be explained, a constitutive explanation describes how the properties of the components and their organization give rise to the system's properties. In both cases the counterfactual criterion prevails: in the causal explanation we are interested in what would have been the case had the antecedent events not taken place, while in the constitutive explanation we are interested in what the system's properties would have been had the components' properties not been what they were. However, Ylikoski (2012) believes that one obtains different explanatory information depending on the explanation applied: a causal explanation results in a causal story about the crucial features of the process that gave rise to the subsequent event, whereas a constitutive explanation informs about how the relations between micro-level properties make possible the whole's properties.

Through this line of reasoning, Ylikoski is not denying that the wholes are as real as their parts. What he does deny is the ontological priority of the whole as far as the explanatory information is concerned and that the whole can have causal effects upon its parts. He suggests that social scientists avoid insisting on the priority of the macro over the micro-level because the location of the issue of the explanatory relevance is a contingent matter that depends on the explananda one is addressing. It is in this context that the micro-foundations obtained via mechanism-based accounts have their merit. These accounts first provide information about the reasons why properties related to macro variables depend on the micro-properties of the parts and second enable the findings to be generalized. In other words, the micro-foundations of mechanism-based accounts act as a bridge between the micro and the macro level. The most well-known micro-foundations are situational mechanisms, which refer to the opportunities provided by structures and culture, action-formation mechanisms, which describe how people's beliefs motivate their courses of action and transformational mechanisms, which show how individual actions produce various intended and unintended social outcomes.

Ylikoskis's approach expresses what Daniel Little (2014) has described as the demand for explaining through micro-foundations. Little provides an argument that tries to overcome the deficiency of reductionism stemming from methodological individualism by stating that social structures influencing social outcomes are only possible in so far as they are embodied in the actions and states of socially constructed individuals. Instead of attributing explanatory power to autonomous social forces, Little believes that all social properties and effects are conveyed through the individuals who constitute a population at a particular time. What he terms "methodological localism" (Little 2014, 61) is but an urge to learn more about how individuals are formed and constituted in concrete, socially structured situations and how actions are structured in local social environments. The main tool available to achieve this goal is the discovery of the underlying causal mechanisms that give rise to outcomes of interest. For Little, social mechanisms are concrete social processes in which a set of social conditions, constraints, or circumstances combine to bring about a given outcome. Instead of hunting for laws discovered by induction, Little gives prominence to the search for specific causal influences and variations by emphasizing variety, contingency and the availability of alternative pathways leading to an outcome.

After this discussion, it is easy for one to grasp how methodological individualists conceive of the possibility of attributing mental states to collectivities. In the same way as one can attribute mental states to an individual in order to interpret his or her behaviour, one is justified in attributing an intentional stance to a collection of individuals in order to interpret their behaviour. They are not ontologically committed to the existence of a collective intentionality, but view it as if it exists in order to make their behaviours intelligible. It is obvious that this approach to collective intentionality is reductionist and instrumental. Joint intentions are considered as a specific, complex "species" of individual mental states and in this sense intentions, beliefs or actions can only have one individual bearer.

Even though methodological individualists approach collective intentionality in a reductive way, the social-theoretical tradition propounding the social grounding of the mind is not without problems. Holistic theories of mind approach the individual mind as a bearer of meanings that is part of a collective mind whose nature is semantic. The location of the semantic mind lies in the public realm of shared meanings and institutions. For Kaufmann (1999), the expression "social mind" is a pleonasm because mind and society are two different parts of the same whole structure, two levels of instantiation of the same object, which is conveniently called "society".

However, holistic approaches are not without their internal divisions regarding the extent to which the mind is individual. For those who subscribe to a Durkheimian view of society, a mild view of emergentism is at work, although not analyzed in much depth, ultimately favouring an essentialist perspective of the society to the extent that the whole causally affects humans and agency is lost. By contrast, holists of the Winch-inspired tradition do not separate mental entities from the concepts that society uses to construct them. In this sense, language is not just a tool for accessing reality, but what makes both mental entities and reality exist. In this line of reasoning, there is no room for emergentism: the mind is populated from society's concepts and humans do not have privileged access to their reasons for action. In other words, while Durkheimians face the objection of dualism, for contractualists of the Winch type mind and society's concepts are conflated. Proponents of a Winch-inspired theory of language believe that the mind is publicly observable and so mental states are no longer a resource of explanation but a theme of investigation. What requires explanation is not reasons for action but how they are constructed within a specific "language game". In this sense, reasons for action do not have causal power because this power is found in the conventions of the community. The reasons for action are not psychological dispositions but exist due to the vocabulary of motives prevalent in a community.

According to this line of thought, it follows that mental states are publicly observable processes and so carry a normative dimension. The publicity of mental states means that they correspond to criteria of appropriateness and correctness of how one should use words in specific contexts (Kaufmann 2010). Mental states are the furniture of the mind that can be described by an external third-person observer. We believe that the main deficiency of this third-person holistic conception of the mind is that it does not offer a specific account of mechanism-based explanations. The task of social science is limited to describing how the social semantics of the mind shape individual thinking and acting. In practice, this has been expressed in the injunction that social researchers should thickly describe webs of meaning in context. This is not a bad thing for social science, but it does not tell us why things exist in one form and not another, or why one theory has more explanatory power than another. The goal of the grammar-inspired conception of the mind is to describe how mental contents are dependent on the conceptual and linguistic ways in which the community refers to those very entities. In this sense, whatever belongs to the external world (social organizations, cultural artefacts) causally affects mental states (reasons for actions). However, Kaufmann (2011) maintains that such a conception is in no way a third-person approach to the collective mind.

Margaret Gilbert's theory of the "plural subject" (2014) represents a solution to these impasses. The "we" is composed of different individuals who mutually commit themselves to joint actions and collective beliefs and readily endorse the deontic rights and obligations linked to this commitment. Through this joint commitment, individuals give up their full authority over their own actions to the group, believe as a single mind and act as "a single body". In Durkheimian words, it is normativity that makes a belief collective in the sense that group members are supposed to accept and publicly endorse the official beliefs of their group, lest they be blamed for not fulfilling their obligations. However, Gilbert's account applies to cases for which a shared intention is reached through joint commitment, personal communication and mutual agreement, but not to large institutions and organizations or to informal consensus and normative expectations. Whereas for Gilbert "we-intentions" are at the centre of attention, large institutions and normative compliance refer to what Kauffman calls the impersonal "one". In such cases, collectives can develop a mind of their own, potentially discontinuous with the mentality of their members. Society comprises "concrete totalities" that are characterized by relational properties that are neither group- nor individual-level properties. Raimo Tuomela and Chrysostomos Mantzavinos provide well-known arguments regarding how collectivities (groups, institutions, and organizations) can have mental states.

Tuomela (2007), in asking whether groups can have a mind of their own, believes that we-mode thinking and acting provides the answer. We-mode is a way of viewing the irreducibility of the social in cases where group members are acting and thinking for a group purpose or are collectively committed to a group task. Collective commitment means that group members bind themselves to an idea, action or to the group itself and carries a normative dimension in a moral, legal or prudential sense. For Tuomela, the concept of we-mode is a holistic institutional notion that aims to tap into what it means for a group member to take the "group's views and commitments as his authoritative reasons for thinking and acting as the group 'requires'" (Tuomela 2007, 14). His theory concerns groups a) with voluntary membership, b) that address a class of topics of concern, c) that develop specific attitudes about these topics and d) that are permeated by an ethos (goals, values, beliefs, standards, norms, practices and/or traditions) that provide the group members with motivating reasons for action. Group members are committed to this ethos and set in motion collective actions to maintain it. Reasons for action are what distinguish the I-mode from the we-mode attitude. The difference lies at what Tuomela (2007, 22) defines as a "collectivity condition". In I-mode, reasons for acting X have a psychological and private content and are only contingently connected to a group reason, while in we-mode, reasons for action are necessarily connected to what one's group has committed itself to in the situation at hand, where the group's commitment serves as an authoritative reason for the participants. If the above conditions are satisfied, one can easily attribute mental states to groups taken to be capable of making judgments and constructing institutions in virtue of collective commitment to the group ethos.

One can however raise an objection to Tuomela's theory of social action. Tuomela accepts that it is conceptually charged agents' thinking that causally affects behaviour, no matter how extra-individual entities interact with agents. He believes that holistic social entities (institutions, groups and their properties) do not really exist and in this sense Tuomela is committed to an ontological individualism. Holistic concepts can be used, but only for functional purposes, as they play a functional role in theoretical explanations. Social events are real if and only if people have appropriate mutual beliefs concerning them. The existence of social events is not really real; their reality is dependent upon agents' beliefs about them. However, Tuomela retains a reconciling attitude as to the objective reality of the external world, because although social entities are dependent upon individualistically construed social practices, they can be studied in their own right without this contradicting an ultimate individualistic scientific realism. The truth is that Tuomela (1984, 3–4) is not preoccupied with analyzing how this reconciliation may be achieved but with proving that "there are no holistic social entities such as groups, institutions and their properties".

A similar line of reasoning can be found in one version of ontological individualism that tries to grasp and explain the genesis of institutions and their raison d'êtres. One of the leading exponents of this version, Mantzavinos (2010) provides a version of ontological individualism which uses intentional explanations for making sense of social phenomena. Although he accepts that meaning-making processes are a constitutive part of the social and that social actions are meaningful, he approaches meaning through the prism of causal explanation and as something that can be explained in a naturalistic manner, rather than through the lens of interpretivism. Instead of reproducing the old-fashioned dualism between Verstehen and Erklären, he proposes that actions are inscribed into a nexus of meaning that can be apprehended through four points of view. First, this nexus refers to an actor's motives that set in motion specific lines of action. Second, it can be apprehended whether the intention of the action is identified. Here, intentions are related to an actor's mental state, like beliefs and desires, with an action representing the final outcome. An elaboration of this, third, is that mental states are an actor's reasons for an action through which nexuses of meaning are made. Finally, the fourth way to make sense of this nexus is an actor's rationality. An actor ranks his or her goals according to his or her preferences and chooses the one that will improve his or her position. An action is the final outcome of how rationality transforms beliefs and desires into a concrete decision. How is this variously defined nexus of meaning transformed into a causal nexus? Simply by stating that an action is caused by the reasons an actor has in mind. Although this line of argument has been criticized as a tautology (Rosenberg 2008), Mantzavinos believes that this is not the case, suggesting that we focus on the regularity dimension of this causal nexus. As he argues,

> [e]very time that one succeeds in identifying similar fundamental elements either in connection with the nexuses of meaning of other actions of the same person or in connection with the nexuses of meaning of the actions of other persons, one has been successful in identifying a regularity.
>
> (Mantzavinos 2010, 6)

For Mantzavinos, what transforms a nexus of meaning into a causal nexus is the similarity of reasons for action, expressed as a social action and resembling the concept of generalizability. Statements that describe regularities in the fundamental elements of the nexuses of meaning constitute "generalizations" rather than genuine "laws". However, he does not provide further elaboration as to how generalizable regularities across cases are causal, for the simple reason that such elaboration is unnecessary. Instead of taking sides in the debate on whether causality is a metaphysical notion that deserves philosophical attention or not, Mantzavinos holds that what matters is the regularity and not whether it is causal or not. Regularity is what transforms a nexus of meaning into a causal nexus. To the extent that one has detected this regularity, then the explanation has been achieved. In other words, Mantzavinos is in favour of a kind of descriptivism because he identifies the explanation with the description of regularities of a nexus of meaning that can be transformed into a causal nexus if and only if these regularities have been identified. Mantzavinos aims to dispute interpretivists' dictum that meanings cannot be viewed through the prism of regularity rather than whether regularities are "laws" in the traditional sense. Although promising, we believe that Mantzavinos' argument fails to distinguish generalization from explanation: it is one thing to say that something is probable and quite another to provide causal details of why this thing took place. Knowledge of the conditions that make the difference is missing from his argument.

What ontological individualists are trying to grapple with concerns how one can conceive of the relation between social facts and facts about individual people. According to what we have said thus far, "facts about individual people" have to do with reasons for action, or a causal nexus in

Mantzavinos' terms. Given that ontological individualism is the thesis that social facts or phenomena are exhaustively built from (or depend on) individualistic counterparts, emergentism has been proposed as a way to overcome the deficiencies of this reductionism. Emergentism describes cases in which lower-level parts interact in ways that upper-level configurations are formed and the properties of which emerge through this interaction. For Kim, emergence describes two things. First, that the properties that emerge in the upper and configurational level cannot be predicted through one's knowledge of the lower-level parts. In this sense, these emergent properties are novel. What is crucial in this idea is that a large proportion of the social phenomena related to the unintended consequences of action owe their existence not to the actors' rationality or reasons for action but to the causal power of the emergent properties of the whole. This is why emergence stands in stark contrast to reductionist explanations, which tend to reduce upper-level phenomena to knowledge of the parts of which they are composed. Second, these emergent properties bear causal power, which is independent from the constituents of the interacting parts and which can shape their behaviour. By contrast, the reductionist views espoused by methodological individualists do not deny the existence of collectives, but believe that their explanations should be reduced to individual properties, be they psychological dispositions or people's reasons for action. In other words, in this kind of reductionism, the macro is explained in terms of micro-properties.

Philosophers of mind have used the term "supervenience" to describe how higher-level entities and properties are grounded on and determined by more basic properties of physical matter. They believe that higher-level properties supervene upon the system of lower-level properties. Supervenience is a philosophical argument composed of two interconnected ideas: first, that if two events are identical with respect to their description at the lower level, then they do not differ at the higher level; second, that an entity cannot change at the higher level without also changing at the lower level. Many philosophers of social science resist admitting the irreducibility of the social by claiming that all higher-level types or properties are identical to lower-level descriptions. In this way, they believe that supervenience is a good friend of the type of identity thesis. In other words, they remain ontological individualists by bringing from the backdoor reductionism through supervenience. Thus, ontological individualism states that social facts supervene on or are exhaustively grounded by individualistic ones. Note here that the supervenience argument is asymmetrical. While an entity at a higher level cannot change without also changing at the lower levels, an entity may change at the lower level and retain the same description at the higher level (Sawyer 2004).

However, philosophers of mind who make use of the supervenience argument have gradually acknowledged that more complex systems cannot be explained through reference to their basic constituents. The fact that two sets of properties co-vary does not prove that one is built out of the other. In order to deal with this problem, an alternative way of grounding the social upon the individual has been crafted: the idea is to state that one fact is the case *in virtue of* another fact being the case. Things start to become difficult for ontological individualists when they try to make sense of "relationships of interaction" or "social structures". It is impossible to make sense of what a person does when he or she takes money from an ATM bank machine without making reference to social or holistic concepts (for example, financial system, bank technology). Supervenience is not a solution because of the unpredictability argument suggested by Kim, which means that supervenience alone cannot sustain the irreducibility of the social.

In order to negotiate the unpredictability of higher-level properties, individualists have made use of the multiple realizability argument. In simple terms, this means that although supervenient, each token instance of any mental state can be realized by a different physical state. At the social level this means that the same reasons for action can give rise to different social wholes. However, according to Fodor (1974), multiple realizability does not lead to the acceptance of irreducibility. Reduction is avoided only in cases that the combinations of lower-level properties are unrelated to the properties of the higher level. In such cases, realization is wildly disjuncted, as Fodor claims. Only in cases of wild disjunction can one sustain the irreducibility of social properties. In other words, to whatever conception of law one subscribes, in cases that a law comprises wildly disjunctive terms, its scientific usefulness is limited because the higher-level phenomena it can explain are limited. As Kincaid (1996) has noted, whenever a social description applies to phenomena that can be brought about in diverse ways by individual behaviour in different situations or at different times, then reductionism is doomed to fail.

Emergentism adds to the idea of supervenience that higher-level entities have causal influence upon the lower-level parts.[1] This kind of causation is a property of emergence processes because such processes emerge simultaneously within different systems at different levels of analysis. Emergent causation may take three directions: upward, downward and the same level. The first means that higher-level entities are explained by lower-level entities; the second means that a lower-level property is instantiated because of the emergent higher-level property; and the third concerns explanations related to entities belonging to the same ontological level (Gorski 2009). Downward and upward causation is described by Kim as follows:

a whole, W, has a certain (emergent) property M; W is constituted by parts, $a1, \ldots, an$, and there are properties $P1, \ldots, Pn$ respectively of $a1, \ldots, an$ and a certain relation R holding for the $a$is. [This means that] (i) [Downward causation] W's having property M causes some aj to have Pj; but (ii) [Upward determination] each ai's having Pi and R holding for the $a$is together determine W to have M – that is, W's having M depends wholly on (or is wholly constituted by) the $a$is having the Pi respectively and being related by R.

(Kim 1999, 27)

In social theoretical circles, many scholars accept that there exist irreducible social properties and social laws, but remain faithful ontological individualists in the sense that they maintain that only individuals exist, while social entities having no distinct existence. They believe that emergence is not necessarily incompatible with reduction to individual-level explanations of social phenomena. Social properties do not have an autonomous existence and cannot have causal power over individuals. Homans' sociological behaviourism, Coleman's rational action theory and Elster's individual emergentism are some of the best-known examples that are still in use. According to these traditions, it is individuals' reasons for action on which social scientists should rely in order to gain access to social entities. This line of thinking, in its Weberian version, states that even though agents often act without a clear awareness of their means and goals, shaped by historical, social and economical configurations, they are typified as if they are rational actors who should have performed the same action in the same circumstances. Reasons for acting should not be identified with utilitarianism, because rational actions can also be "axiological" and value-laden. In other words, those who adopt the above line of thought succumb to a mild version of methodological holism, but they are ontological individualists regarding the *sui generis* existence of social entities. As Kaufmann (2011) underlines, they accept the compositional criterion of social wholes (social entities exist because they are composed of individuals) but not the causal (social entities are not causally efficacious). One should not forget that these weaker versions of methodological individualism share a first-person perspective of the human mind because they prioritize both to the privileged access actors have to their mental states through introspection and to the infallible knowledge that stems from it.[2]

In contrast to what we have said thus far regarding how methodological individualists prefer to causally explain the social by reducing it to individuals and their reluctance to attribute causal force to the wholes, we tend to believe that one can detect causal mechanisms not at the individual level but at the level of the wholes. One basic idea of this holistic picture is that, instead of taking at face value individuals' beliefs and desires, one should strive to explain how they have been formed. Individual behaviour has causes and constraints far beyond what appears as apparent to commonsense psychology. Despite the fact that individualists' preference for reductive explanations aims to eliminate social explanations, their main weakness is that reduction presupposes 1) a connection of the description at the individual level with the description at the social level and 2) that this connection must be able to explain what happens at the social level. Reduction fails because there are no descriptions connecting the individual with the social. The core idea of ontological individualists is that because wholes consist of and do not act independently of their parts, it follows that they can neither cause nor determine them. However, according to Kincaid (1996), while a social entity S may be composed entirely of individuals Ii, Iii ..... In and not act independently of them, it does not follow that our theory of Ii, Iii ..... In lacks the power to capture higher-level explanations. It is one thing that people do not get married in order to reproduce the nuclear family and it is quite another that the nuclear family emerged only under specific social conditions (for example, industrialization, division of labour) and not others (medieval economy).

Bhaskar (1998, 29) dispenses with explaining the social in "plural" terms: given that an army is composed of soldiers, one can reduce statements about the army to statements about the soldiers comprising it. In contrast to this, he holds that all the predicates referring to specific persons presuppose a social context for their application. A coach implies a basketball club and the cashing of a cheque a banking system. Explanation always irreducibly involves social predicates for the simple reason that sociology is concerned with relations between people and with relations of the relations.

We believe that the main deficiency with how ontological and methodological individualists make sense of causality is that they either presuppose social wholes or use them for explanatory reasons without providing a sufficient theoretical framing of them or without acknowledging their causal efficiency. The reason for this deficiency is that individualists try to make sense of the reducibility of the social through the multiple realization argument. The problem is that whenever such an argument is put in practice without the addition of wild disjunction, social wholes or social concepts (social roles, relations, organizations) are presupposed in the individualists' descriptions with the effect that social explanations are not eliminated.

Let us give two examples of how this happens in social science. Let us suppose that the social phenomenon S1 (say, the emergence of lifelong learning institutions) is connected with the reason for action 1 (say RfA 1=desire for self-realization), the reason for action 2 (say RfA 2= occupational improvement) and the reason for action 3 (say RfA 3= find a job).

One cannot reduce S1 to these multiple RfAs without a bridging theory capable of explaining how different RfAs (1,2,3...n) can give rise to S1. In addition, it is possible that one of these RfAs (for example RfA 1) can give rise to a different S2 (say, increased divorce) and/or S3 (creation of counselling services). This means that a social property may be said to be emergent when it is multiply realized in wildly disjunctive social relations. In this way, reductionism fails because there are no criteria for distinguishing real from spurious causation. The same holds for the role the context plays in influencing social phenomena. For example, when Hedström (2005) talks about situations that limit desires and opportunities, he makes use of a context-sensitive individual description but only presupposes (rather than theorizes) this context.

Philosophers of mind have provided a solution to these issues by constructing an argument similar to Durkheim's theory of emergentism, albeit stated in their own parlance. They argue that due to wildly disjunctive multiple realizability, it may be the case that a social property S with a supervenience base A at time t1 can be identified as the cause of social property S1 and the individual property A1 at time t2. This means that methodological individualists' aspiration to forge lawful explanations with reference to lower-level properties is futile. As Sawyer (2002) notes, disjunctive lower-level properties are not causal properties. On the contrary, social properties can be causal in the following sense: a social property S at time t1 causes individual property A2 at time 2 even though supervenience base A1 at time t1 does not lawfully cause A2 or social property S1 at time t2.

A way out of this impasse is to explain social phenomena not as types but as tokens, that is, as particular and specific events localized in time and space. For example, instead of explaining the event type "financial crisis", a token-event approach prioritizes the explanation of the financial crisis in Greece between 2009 and 2018. In the case of approaching social events as tokens, the explanation is made on a case-by-case basis and the causality is singular. Weber's singular causality is the best-known implementation of the token-event explanation. Briefly stated, causality is singular when one identifies the specific conditions that mediate between an antecedent and a consequent event (Ringer 1997). In this case, we are not dealing with what is called "invariable succession" between two types of events, one of which is the cause and the other is the effect, but with tracing the anterior conditions that increase the probability of a given result taking place. What matters in this causal reasoning is the tapping of conditions that make the difference. The cause changes the course of events in the sense that had this specific cause not existed, then a divergent course of events would have been the case. In other words, the absence of the cause would have been followed by a divergent course of events. According to such causal thinking, the results would have been different had the cause not occurred. Although this counterfactually conceived singular causality is not holistic, we regard it as a powerful explanatory tool because it prioritizes the identification of the specific causal process leading from the antecedent event A to the subsequent event B and not C. In any case, we hold that this conception of causation is close to the three basic tenets proposed by Bunge (2006) regarding what it means to causally explain something: first, that a causal relation is asymmetric in the sense that causes bring about effects, not vice versa; second that a causal relation is obtained between events; and, third, that causal relations hold only among changes. From these three tenets, Bunge provides a definition of causation of use to qualitative researchers due to the role it ascribes to causal chains and processes conceived as an "energy transfer" connecting changes related to two events:

> Event C in thing A causes event E in thing B if and only if the occurrence of C generates an energy transfer from A to B resulting in the occurrence of E.
>
> (Bunge 2006, 91)

We think that this analysis enables the reader to understand why mechanism-based explanations fit with qualitative research and in particular with biographical research: first, because causality most of times in qualitative research is singular; and, second, because the level at which the mechanisms are to be detected is not belief formation or social situations, but the configurational structure permeating the parts of higher-order entities. This is why in Chapters 5–9 of the book we try to show how CR can become the philosophical background so that one can claim causal explanations using biographical research. The parts of an entity can be approached through two perspectives. First, as inter-substituted parts that are interchangeable and that may be added one after the other, meaning that regardless of how the parts are interconnected, the outcome will always be the same. Indeed, the properties of the whole are disrupted only when and if some parts are added or removed. Second, as components of a mechanism, with specific properties emerging from the configuration. Although this conception of mechanistic emergence does not guarantee the irreducibility of the social, it promotes a hierarchical conception of the part/whole relation that is more appropriate for studying social phenomena and in particular for identifying inter-level causation. One of the ideas sustaining this conception and that deserves to be used for our purposes is that the properties of the whole cannot be predicted from the properties of the parts.

For Glennan (2017), mechanisms are composed of lower-order entities and activities and are parts of the furniture of the causal structure of the world. Both of them under specific conditions and under specific configurations do something and hence have powers that are causally effective. Or else, the form through which parts are organized makes social entities have causal effects. This is close to a system-inspired approach to causation. At the same time, the activity sustaining the relation of the parts enables one to tap the temporal nature of causation and to conceive of it as a process. Glennan's approach to causality is ontological and asks what kinds of things are causes or relata and what conditions must be fulfilled so that the cause can be connected with an outcome. There is a crucial ontological difference between the singular and the universalistic conception of a mechanism. For the latter, a singular causal claim holds only because it realizes a universal law, whereas for the former, it holds because the context matters. This is an additional reason why we believe the singular conception of a mechanism-based explanation is congruent with biographical research. From this conception, two kinds of causation come to the fore: first, causes produce and bring about effects; second, causes are what make the difference to effects. The first kind is of a singular nature because it concerns a continuity between causes and effects, while the second has the merit of approaching causes and effects on a comparative basis. We believe that it is not by accident that Glennan, not a social theorist but a philosopher of life sciences, provides an account of singular causality that could only have been offered by a biographical researcher. In order to clarify why generalizations are not the kind of explanations sought by the social sciences, he offers the following example:

> What causes an individual to become a terrorist or a priest or a winemaker is the product of the very particular history of that individual. We may be able to make statistical generalizations about the relationships between these properties, but such generalizations are simply local summaries of correlations among populations of heterogeneous individuals. The generalizations may be of local use, but they will not be projectable to different times or places. And these generalizations, while they may fallibly predict, will not explain. If we are really to understand what causes an individual to do anything, we must look at the particular properties and circumstances of that individual.
>
> (Glennan 2017, 4–5)

Producing or generating outcomes through specific pathways or processes is too close to the conception of singular causation developed by Glennan. This means that causal mechanisms are sufficient for outcomes to take place; in Chapter 4 we provide details concerning how this can be achieved according to process-tracing theorists. In addition, these theorists have provided insightful approaches regarding what happens when a causal mechanism prevents something from taking place or, in other words, when causal mechanisms prevent outcomes from occurring. These mechanisms have tended to be identified with the necessary conditions of why something takes place (or not). We deem this an additional reason why biographical research can provide privileged access to the sufficient and necessary conditions of social phenomena. In particular, biographical research can offer access first to the specific scope conditions within which causal mechanisms are triggered and second to how these causal mechanisms are connected with each other, or to what is called "causal configuration". According to this mechanism-based explanation, causal mechanisms involve high degrees of regularity, but are not without exceptions. According to the set-theoretic logic, this means that contexts make the difference because they trigger mechanisms' activation, with causality tied to degrees of membership, not just the absence or presence of causes and effects. However, as we argue in Chapter 5, the most decisive frame for achieving generality through biographical research is case selection.

Be that as it may, making reference to holistic concepts is a *sine qua non* condition for explaining causally social facts. In Chapter 4 we present a more detailed account of the causality-as-process-tracing approach to causal explanation connected with Mackie's INUS condition. We believe that individualists end up being reductionists because of their desire for a unified theory of causality in social science. In contrast to this, we maintain that one can achieve causal explanations in social science without succumbing to shortcomings such as those analyzed in this chapter. A backbone idea of this book is that this can be realized by bringing CR in contact with the process-tracing approach to causality.

Notes

1 Although those who adopt relational emergentism reject the explanatory primacy of lower-level entities, they acknowledge the necessity of formulating a theory of the subject. As we have already mentioned, emergentism is not identical with holism, because higher-level entities supervene upon lower-level components. The difference from reductive individualism is that complex systems (as societies) resist reductionist analysis notwithstanding supervenience.

2 Ontological individualists are emergentists because they acknowledge the existence of emergent social properties but maintain that these properties are merely analytical constructs. The explanatory work is done by lower-level properties. On the other hand, the relational emergentism we defend in this book is in favour of a stratified social ontology (see the chapter on critical realism) for which social entities supervene upon individuals, but each stratum is ontologically autonomous and real and not an analytical construct. For Sawyer (2005), the only solid

ground of relational emergentists' realist claims about higher-level entities is that many social properties are multiply realized by wild disjunction. On the basis of this line of thought, relational emergentists hold that social properties are causally effective in the sense that their causation is not reducible to individuals even though the causal power of the causal property lies in its individual supervenience.

References

Bhaskar, R. *The Possibility of Naturalism. A Philosophical Critique of the Contemporary Human Sciences*. 3rd ed. London and New York: Routledge, 1998.

Bunge, M. *Chasing Reality: Strife over Realism*. Toronto: University of Toronto Press, 2006.

Coleman, S.J. *Foundations of Social Theory*. Cambridge, MA: Harvard University Press, 1994.

Epstein, B. "What Is Individualism in Social Ontology? Ontological Individualism vs. Anchor Individualism." In *Rethinking the Individualism-Holism Debate. Essays in the Philosophy of Social Science*, edited by J. Zahle, and F. Collin, 17–39. London: Springer, 2014.

Fodor, J. "Special Sciences (or: the Disunity of Science as a Working Hypothesis)." *Synthese* 28, no. 2 (1974): 97–115. http://www.jstor.org/stable/20114958.

Gilbert, M. *Joint Commitment How We Make the Social World*. Oxford: Oxford University Press, 2014.

Glennan, S. *The New Mechanical Philosophy*. Oxford: Oxford University Press, 2017.

Gorski, P. "Social 'Mechanisms' and Comparative-Historical Sociology: A Critical Realist Proposal." In *Frontiers of Sociology*, edited by P. Hedström, and B. Wittrock, 147–94. Leiden/Boston: Brill, 2009.

Hedström, P. *Dissecting the Social. On the Principles of Analytical Sociology*. Cambridge: Cambridge University Press, 2005.

Kaufmann, L. "Esprit, es-tu là? Le sociologue et l'autorité de la première personne". *Information sur les Sciences Sociales* 38, no. 2 (1999): 203–48. doi:10.1177/053901899038002002.

Kaufmann, L. "Faire collectif: de la constitution à la maintenance." *Raisons Pratiques* 20 (2010): 331–72.

Kaufmann, L. "Social Minds." In *The Sage Handbook of the Philosophy of Social Sciences*, edited by I.C. Jarvie, and J. Zamora-Bonilla, 53–82. London: Sage Publications, 2011.

Keat, R., and J. Urry. *Social Theory as Science*. London and New York: Routledge, 1975.

Kim, J. "Making Sense of Emergence." *Philosophical Studies* 95, no. 1/2 (1999): 3–36.

Kincaid, H. *Philosophical Foundations of the Social Sciences. Analyzing Controversies on Social Research*. Cambridge: Cambridge University Press, 1996.

Little, D. "Explanatory Autonomy and Coleman's Boat". *THEORIA. An International Journal for Theory, History and Foundations of Science* 27, no. 2 (2012): 137–51. doi:10.1387/theoria.3016.

Little, D. "Actor-Centered Sociology and the New Pragmatism." In *Rethinking the Individualism-Holism Debate. Essays in the Philosophy of Social Science*, edited by J. Zahle, and F. Collin, 55–77. London: Springer, 2014.

Mantzavinos, C. "Explanations of Meaningful Actions." *Philosophy of the Social Sciences* 42, no. 2 (2010): 1–15. doi:10.1177/0048393110392590.

Ringer, F. *Max Weber's Methodology: The Unification of the Cultural and Social Sciences*. Cambridge: Harvard University Press, 1997.

Rosenberg, A. *Philosophy of Social Science*. 3rd ed. Philadelphia: Westview Press, 2008.

Sawyer, R.K. "Nonreductive Individualism: Part I - Supervenience and Wild Disjunction." *Philosophy of the Social Sciences* 32, no. 4 (2002): 537–59. doi:10.1177/004839302237836.

Sawyer, R.K. "The Mechanisms of Emergence." *Philosophy of the Social Sciences* 34, no. 2 (2004): 260–85. doi:10.1177/0048393103262553.

Sawyer, R.K. *Social Emergence. Societies as Complex Systems*. Cambridge: Cambridge University Press, 2005.

Tuomela, R. *A Theory of Social Action*. Dordrecht: Reidel Publishing Company, 1984.

Tuomela, R. *The Philosophy of Sociality. The Shared Point of View*. Oxford: Oxford University Press, 2007.

Ylikoski, P. "Micro, Macro, and Mechanism." In *The Oxford Handbook of Philosophy of Social Science*, edited by H. Kincaid, 21–45. Oxford: Oxford University Press, 2012.

Ylikoski, P. "Causal and Constitutive Explanation Compared." *Erkenntnis* 78, no. 2 (2013): 277–97. doi:10.1007/s10670-013-9513-9.

3 Critical realism

Causal mechanisms as emergent powers

Critical realism (CR) is a philosophy of social science that is differentiated from the two best-known philosophies of science, Hume's empirical realism and Kant's transcendental idealism. In reading Bhaskar's theory, the noted scholar who established CR as a distinct philosophical tradition, one gets the sense that his main opponent is Humean philosophy rather than hermeneutics or phenomenology. We believe the reason is that CR acknowledges how social phenomena exist due to people's reasons for action and meaning attribution, hence social reality is always already pre-interpreted by agents before a scientist tries to make sense of it. However, CR disputes interpretivists' phenomenalism by stating that a) the reasons for action take place within material and cultural conditions and b) social life has a non-propositional dimension in the sense that agents experience the world in an embodied manner. In this way, while CR accepts (in line with hermeneutics) the concept-dependent foundation of the social, it aspires to identify its causal explanation and so its philosophical foundations are not phenomenalism but emergent systemism (Bunge 1979).

The social theories deriving from the main philosophical traditions of the 19th century had to deal with an intriguing puzzle that continues to haunt social theorists today, regardless of whether one approaches it through an epistemological or an ontological lens: namely, how can something that is concept-dependent (social reality) be an object of knowledge, given that scientists use concepts in order to access it? The "classic" figures of social theory were puzzled about this issue, which concerns the conditions of possibility that make a science of society possible. In order to resolve this puzzle, CR draws upon the known realist idea that there exists a world independent of how we think of it and that our knowledge of it is fallible exactly because of this independency. Given that this idea has been accused of circularity, Bhaskar provides three ground-breaking ideas for overcoming it.

First, he repeatedly denotes that the objects of science constitute one thing while the theories scientists forge to grasp them represent something entirely else (Bhaskar 1998). Even though our theories of the social world are socially and historically contingent and are subject to social influences, the social world itself has an ontological independency from the social scientific field in which these theories are formed. This is the well-known distinction between the transitive and the intransitive dimensions of knowledge. Despite the fact that social theories are socially constructed, this does not mean that there are no theories that are more truthful than others. The main disagreement of Bhaskar's CR with direct realism is that the latter is based on the representative model of knowledge, the ontology of which accepts the existence of discrete individual events which are known through sense experiences (Bhaskar 2008). It is only in this world that Hume's constant conjunctions between A and B obtain their meaning, with causality nothing but these conjunctions. It is not by accident that the use of experimental methods in social science has been based upon this conception of causality to which Bhaskar is opposed.

Second, the best-known idea Bhaskar has put forward concerns how the social world is made up of three separate but interconnected strata: the real, in which mechanisms and processes are identified; the actual, referring to what is happening regardless of whether agents are aware of it; and the empirical, or what agents experience. The Real is about how generative mechanisms give shape to the world's objects and affect the other two strata. For CR, the aim of social research is to identify the necessary and sufficient conditions that make things happen and produce outcomes. The actual refers to the events that happen if and only if these conditions and powers are triggered and the empirical concerns what is experienced by individuals. Thus, it follows that the observable is quite distinct from what exists. For CR, social reality is not limited to what actors perceptually experience, that is, only to the "empirical" level of reality. Rather, social reality is also composed of social events (the "actual" level), of which existence is not dependent upon actors' perceptions. The conditions of possibility for both the empirical and the actual to take place through specific forms are provided by the generative mechanisms at work in the "real" level (Bhaskar 2008; 1998). The philosophical innovation of this stratified social ontology is twofold. First, although it acknowledges the concept-dependent dimension of social reality, it gives precedence to the independent existence of generative mechanisms that emerge in the "actual" and in the "real" ontological levels. Second, although controversial in philosophical circles, the concept of "emergence" is fundamental should one choose to make sense of CR.

The third idea proposed by Bhaskar draws upon the philosophical struggles regarding "emergence" we analyzed in the first chapter. Bhaskar thinks that when A and B interact, then C emerges, whose properties – despite coming from A's and B's properties – differ in terms of logic and have something to say regarding why C has taken that form and not another. C's emergent properties are not reducible to the lower-level properties even though they exist because of them. What Bhaskar underlines is that the emergent properties are not closed systems but rather are always open to change and transformation.

Bhaskar devotes a large part of his energy to undermining Hume's regularity conception of causality, which frames experimental methods and which he deems inappropriate for social science. It follows that the same holds for the qualitative research. His main disagreement is that this conception assumes that regularity exists only in so far as the scientist is aware of it, otherwise there is no constant conjunction. Bhaskar believes that his disagreement with Hume can be summarized in two contrasting questions. Whereas CR asks "how the social world must be in order for science to be possible", thereby assuming that the world is a necessary condition for science to be possible, Hume's empiricism asks "how science should be in order for its knowledge to be justified" (Bhaskar 2008, 26–7). The first question acknowledges the social production of science, whereas the second conceives of scientific operation in asocial terms. This is the reason why empiricism transforms ontological issues into epistemological issues and makes sense data the ultimate arbiter of truth. By contrast, for Bhaskar what we know (knowledge) comes after what exists (existence) logically and temporally.

Bhaskar's conceptualization of the furniture of the social world is an alternative to both phenomenalism and holism, as he prioritizes emergence as an ontological category. Bunge (2003) has provided an accurate account of the relationality of the social that is quite similar to Bhaskar's, starting with the premise that there are two ways in which things can relate to one another: either through association and concatenation or through combination. In association, things are joined together in a modular way in the sense that their cohesion is low and they can alter or be altered rather easily. In the associationist mode, the part/whole relation is of the following type: A is a part of B despite the fact that A adds nothing to B. Thus, when A and B associate with each other, the nature of the constituents of the association does not change. By contrast, in the combinatory type of relation, when two things interact a radically novel thing emerges, characterized by properties that the constituents of the combination lack. In other words, the combinatory mode of relation is not aggregative in nature. Combinations differ from mere aggregates in at least three regards. First, what constitutes the relation of A and B is not A and B separately but the emergent properties of the relation itself that have the power to affect the precursors; that is, A and B. Second, combinations are more stable than mere aggregates because they are more cohesive. Third, combinations need time to produce the new novelty. The most crucial aspect of combinations is that the wholes resulting from lower-level units have properties that their parts or precursors lack. For example, a valid reasoning (argument) is a system whose conclusion is not included in its separate premises. In this sense, wholes are not similar to their parts and so their properties are called "emergent". These systemic properties originate in the interrelations among the constituents of the systems concerned. From the above it follows that emergence has two meanings: first, emergence is used to describe the qualitatively novel upper-level thing borne out of the relation of two lower-level things (the ontological meaning); second, it is used to denote that the occurrence of the emergent is unpredictable (the epistemological meaning). In other words, a property of a complex object is said to be emergent if neither of the constituents or precursors of the object possesses it. For Bunge (2003), there are no properties by themselves and independently of the things to which they are attached. In addition, there are neither negative nor disjunctive properties, since, Bunge holds, we may truly say of a person that she is not a smoker, but she does not possess the property of being a non-smoker any more than she possesses the property of being a non-whale. Hence, the right thing is not to ask how properties emerge but rather how emergent properties arise. This leads to searching for mechanisms.

Emergence is tied up with a stratified ontology in which the world's furniture is composed of levels. A level is not a thing but a collection of things with certain properties in common. Levels are ordered in a hierarchical way. Given that emergence is related to qualitative novelty for each level, it follows that each level's properties cannot be predicted by reference to the lower level. This does not mean that the more complex levels are ontologically independent from the simpler ones. As Bunge notes, "there is no emergence ex nihilo: everything emerges from something, such as interactions among either the constituents of a system or some of them and environmental items" (Bunge 2003, 28). He also acknowledges what Simmel had previously remarked about the dyad and the triad regarding the three roles that the third party can play when interacting with the dyad. Bunge holds that the relational emergence such as that proposed by Simmel concerns cases where a thing's property may be acquired by virtue of being incorporated into a system. Note also that what may emerge is not only things but also processes and that emergence entails temporality and submergence. In simple terms, this means that emergence needs time to occur, such that the developmental processes and some of the properties of things are lost. From these ontological postulates it follows that one cannot remain indifferent to the relational properties that emerge in various levels. The most crucial aspect of emergence or of the details of each level's properties has to do with structure. In other words, the form of relation matters because it is upon these forms that each level's properties depend: the form of the relation between the constituents of each level defines its properties. A key question concerns whether and how this form is bonding and causal as far as the relata are concerned. This is an issue that needs to be investigated through social research rather than taken as a given. Finally, the ontology of emergence entails the concept of mechanisms, which Bunge defines as follows: "A mechanism is a set of processes in a system, such that they bring about or prevent some change – either the emergence of a property or another process – in the system as a whole" (Bunge 2003, 31).

In a similar vein and in contrast to Hume's phenomenalism, Bhaskar (1998) holds that causal forces and mechanisms exist and work independently of whether agents are aware of them and so they are intransitive and independent of humans' actions. Hence, events are independent of the meaningful experiences through which agents make sense of them. In this sense, mechanisms, events and experiences constitute the three interconnected ontological domains we referred to before: the real, the actual and the empirical, respectively.

Critical realists' approach to causality is in the opposite direction to this sense-data empiricism and counter-proposes that an outcome/event/phenomenon is explained only if a mechanism is identified by detailing why it takes this form and not another as well as by stating clearly the (necessary and sufficient) conditions within which mechanisms' powers are implemented. Causality as regularity presupposes closed systems while causality as mechanism-based processes refers to society's openness. Critical realists explore the necessary and sufficient conditions in which a mechanism is operating and ask about the properties an object/event/situation/institution possesses so that specific outcomes through specific causal processes are produced. Real causal forming forces are emergent properties of social configurations through which the parts of the whole are connected. Here are two aspects that one should bear in mind when assessing causal forces: first, even though they are instantiated to the singulars that make up the events, their sources are real; second, they do not produce exceptionless regularities but tendencies and possibilities. In a critical realist epistemology, instead of searching for regularities, one is trying to identify necessary and sufficient conditions and to specify the social phenomenon, instantiated in various ways.

We think that this conception of causality agrees with Gerring's attempt to provide a unifying definition of causation when he states that "causes refer to events or conditions that raise the probability of some outcome occurring" (Gerring 2005, 169). In this way, causation is framed in probabilistic and not deterministic terms, as formal causes display necessary and efficient conditions for something to happen or change. Thus conceived, a causal explanation should refer to generative mechanisms deployed in the emergent level of the real. Instead of treating actors' reasons for an action as efficient causes, CR views them as the first step for detecting causal mechanisms and for crafting causal propositions.

Let us reconstruct at this point a crucial difference between critical realists and rational action theorists, pertaining to how these two theoretical currents approach the mechanism-based causal explanation. For critical realists, causality is to be found on the emergent level of social relations, as they are developed between the parts of a whole and of which the configuration presents specific emergent properties. By contrast, for rational action theorists, mechanisms are to be found not at the relation level but in individual decision-making processes. Even though the terminology of mechanism-based accounts sounds similar, there exist marked differences between these lines of reasoning. For rational action theorists, something is explained when one can offer satisfying answers to the following questions:

What: The researcher is called to adequately describe the event or the phenomenon and its beginning and final states;

Why: The researcher identifies the causal necessity to which the event is subsumed; and

How: The researcher highlights the causal mechanism at the micro-level that clearly describes the route from the beginning to the final states.

This is how physicists conceive of explanations and apply them to physical phenomena, as the "how" causal mechanism is subsumed under the covering law of "why": for instance, the causal mechanism explaining how the elements of water move is subsumed under the law of physics.

In a completely contrary way, critical realists prioritize the identification of the generative mechanism that causes a specific configuration (relation between parts) to take a specific form. Reasons for actions and individual decision making are unable to explain the social because to the extent that agents' reasons for actions are given *ex post facto*, then they are not the causes of action. According to Elder-Vass (2010), we consciously make decisions, but these do not fully explain the causes of action because a) there is a time lapse between thinking and acting and b) we are always incomplete as to the details of the action. Critical realists disagree, contending that causality is identical with the scheme belief + desire = action because agents' rationality is perturbed by factors such as values, traditions, emotions or fatigue. As Parri (2014) has argued, instrumental rationality is jeopardized because agents have neither the time nor the resources to collect and process information about situations that are uncertain, dilemmatic or mysterious.

Given that society is expressed through the sum of relations within which individuals and groups stand and of which individuals are not always aware, it follows that critical realists aspire to explain the relational nature of agents' lived realities and their properties. Instead of looking for the micro-foundations identified with the parts of the whole, critical realists examine how the causal power of a relation is exercised. Agents' reasons for action are causally effective only because of the properties connected to the relations in which they live their lives. Reasons for action are always already embedded into relations of which the properties are causally effective and trigger these reasons and not others. Note that this relational nature of sociology is at odds both with the Durkheimian emphasis on groups and with the Weberian emphasis on the meaningfulness of action. By contrast, critical realists put at the forefront how the forms of social relations have a causal power upon agents' lived experiences. This means that intentionality depends upon the social forms that make it necessary. People's actions have both intended and unintended consequences exactly because of the peculiarity of these social forms and of the relations developed between them.

This is where the difference between individualists' and critical realists' conceptions of a mechanism-based explanation lies. In contrast to Hedström's (2005) individualist approach to a mechanism-based explanation that focuses on the connections between observable events, the critical realist approach explains *how* a given correlation works, rather than merely *that* such an association is statistically significant. The difference lies in the fact that in the individualistic framework, mechanisms are the derivatives of covering laws based on deductive reasoning, while for critical realists, generative mechanisms supply the real basis for causal laws. In contrast to what happens in closed systems, in societies, generative mechanisms always exist in the plural and thus operate in interplay with one another. In addition, they are real not heuristic tools that enable one to detect links between observable events. Donati (2015) separates mechanistic mechanisms (mechanisms of an aggregative type like those proposed by pragmatists and individualists) from relational mechanisms (mechanisms of a relational type like those proposed by critical realists). In the first case, the effects of mechanisms have an aggregative nature, that is, one that derives from prior dissemination and results from the simple addition of single units (e.g. individuals), while in the second case, relational mechanisms produce emergent effects, generating a new social form with a different relationality among its elements. This is where the role of temporality comes to the fore. In particular, Bhaskar thinks that higher-level entities are explained with reference to the previous processes of the formation of social relations. As he claims, higher-order entities are explained in terms of the principles governing the elements out of which they are formed (diachronic explanatory reduction), compatible with synchronic emergence (Bhaskar 1998).

According to Donati (2015), aggregation looks like a statistical phenomenon that does not require reference to interpersonal relations. If the latter are involved, they figure merely as a social mechanism of attraction/repulsion. Within this line of reasoning, belief-formation mechanisms rest on behaviourist assumptions. Behind this aggregative conception of mechanisms lies the Weberian view of the social action according to which a relation is social because the ego refers him/herself to the alter and vice versa, but there is no reality that emerges from this reciprocal symbolic reference between individuals and the meaning alter attributes to an action. On the contrary, social forms are context-sensitive and reflexivity-based phenomena. A relational mechanism is found at the structure of the relation between events that is the cause of the outcomes and is expressed to the relational feedback that affects how agents operate as parts of the form of the relation, not as isolated agents. The relational feedback restructures the previous we-relation "by changing, for example, their mutual expectations or any of the elements and relations that form the structure of that we-relation" (Donati 2015, 76). It is one thing to conceive of relations as the aggregative outcome of belief-formation imitation mechanisms and quite another to conceive of them as presenting irreducible properties and powers. In the first case, the ego and the alter react to each other's single actions, while in the second they react to the relation between them. Relational feedback for Donati means that agents act in such a way as to adapt to states or conditions of the relation, not to the singular behaviour of others, as Weber maintained and, in this sense, relational feedback is liable to generate other relations. As Donati claims, "agents act on the relation itself as a reality that co-implicates them in one way or another, for good or evil" (Donati 2015, 74). The causal power of relational feedback is that of reorganizing agents in a different configuration of relationship. Relational feedback is a second-order, non-automatic, generative mechanism that operates on a previous we-relation.

Elder-Vass (2014) has developed Bhaskar's argument on the relational nature of sociology's object of study by stating that the relations between the parts of any given whole provide a bridge between one compositional level of entities and the next. These relations are the input for the properties of the whole that are not explained when one explains the intrinsic (that is, non-relational) properties of the parts. The role of science is to provide explanations as to how these interactions produce emergent causal powers and to identify the mechanisms that produce the higher-level powers. Entities have causal power exactly because of their relational nature, which could not be exercised were they not organized into such a whole. He is in favour of a weak kind of emergence in the sense that social scientists need agents' reasons for action in order to trace the properties of the whole, in contrast both to reductive eliminationists who consider higher-level properties as unnecessary and to the traditional functionalistic and structuralistic social theories for which agents' reasons are either unnecessary or "spontaneous sociologies". Beliefs and desires are causally effective for critical realists, otherwise there would be no social entities. However, on the other hand, it is social wholes that explain agents' intentionality. As he suggests,

> [w]eak reductions do not entail that the property being explained or the entity possessing the property can be eliminated from a viable explanation of the effects of the property; whereas strong reductions are explanations of such a property made entirely in terms that are compatible with the non-existence of the whole structured entity.
>
> (Elder-Vass 2014, 47)

In other words, the concept of emergence proposed by critical realists is necessary in order to inform us of the kinds of causal influence the wholes exert upon the parts and how this process takes place. This brings us to the core issue of critical realists' conception of causality: their account for social structure. The kinds of entities that are at work when one talks about the causal power of social structures are two: first, social organizations and institutions, of which the causal power depends on how their role-sets are interrelated; and second, normatively standardized practices (norm circles), which can be defined as a recognizable pattern of either behaviour or action that occurs repeatedly in a social space. Elder-Vass (2010, 195) thinks that norm circles are what enable social institutions to exert their normative influence. Indeed, according to an extended definition he provides, a norm circle

> is the group of people that are committed to endorsing and enforcing a specific norm, a specific standard of observable behaviour. The relation between them that gives them the collective capability to influence behaviour – a greater influence than an unconnected group of individuals would have – is the sense of shared commitment they have to supporting the norm. The members of a norm circle may be unaware of the full extent of the group, and they may not even think of it as a group, but they are generally aware when they act in support of a norm that they are not simply expressing a purely idiosyncratic personal attachment to a particular standard of behaviour. Rather, they are aware that

when they do so they are endorsing a standard that others also endorse, and often do so with the expectation that others would support and approve of their action. The individual, in other words, has a sense, however vague and minimal, that she is acting on behalf of something wider than herself when she acts in support of a norm, and that sense increases the likelihood that she will act in its support, by comparison with the isolated individual with a purely personal attachment to the standard of behaviour concerned.

Elder-Vass seems to be close to the kind of causation invoked by Sawyer (2005), who states that even though individuals are causally effective, they have social properties that are not reducible to their individuality. Once again, the multiple realizability argument is at work: diverse combinations of low-level properties have similar causal impacts by giving birth to the same types of social structure. However, the similarity of causal impacts is not explained by individuals' properties, but through the higher-level properties that exist across their multiple configurations. The causal power of the norm circle is to be found in the social form of the relations between agents within this circle, not to the separate individuals comprising it, no matter how this causal power is exercised. Given that the generative mechanisms critical realists discuss concern social processes through which social outcomes and events are produced, we believe that their conception of causality is very close to those who see causality as process tracing. In the next chapter we present this approach.

References

Bhaskar, R. *The Possibility of Naturalism. A Philosophical Critique of the Contemporary Human Sciences*. 3rd ed. London and New York: Routledge, 1998.

Bhaskar, R. *A Realist Theory of Science*. London and New York: Routledge, 2008.

Bunge, M. *Treatise on Basic Philosophy. Vol. 4: A World of Systems*. Boston: Reidel, 1979.

Bunge, M. *Emergence and Convergence: Qualitative Novelty and the Unity of Knowledge*. Toronto: University of Toronto Press, 2003.

Donati, P. "Social Mechanisms and Their Feedbacks: Mechanical vs Relational Emergence of New Social Formations." In *Generative Mechanisms Transforming the Social Order*, edited by M. Archer, 65–95. New York: Springer, 2015.

Elder-Vass, D. *The Causal Power of Social Structures. Emergence, Structure and Agency*. Cambridge: Cambridge University Press, 2010.

Elder-Vass, D. "Social Entities and the Basis of Their Powers." In *Rethinking the Individualism-Holism Debate. Essays in the Philosophy of Social Science*, edited by J. Zahle, and F. Collin, 39–55. London: Springer, 2014.

Gerring, J. "Causation: A Unified Framework for the Social Sciences." *Journal of Theoretical Politics* 17, no. 2 (2005): 163–98. doi:10.1177/0951629805050859.

Hedström, P. *Dissecting the Social. On the Principles of Analytical Sociology.* Cambridge: Cambridge University Press, 2005.

Parri, L. *Explanation in the Social Sciences. A Theoretical and Empirical Introduction.* Italy: Rubbettino Press, 2014.

Sawyer, R.K. *Social Emergence. Societies as Complex Systems.* Cambridge: Cambridge University Press, 2005.

4 Causal explanation as process tracing

The counterfactually based conception of singular causality we mentioned in the first chapter is at odds with the Hempelian paradigm of initial conditions and deductive-nomological explanations and is more in line with Salmon's approach to causality. According to Salmon, what matters when one provides an explanation to "why" questions is to give causal details about processes relating to how something happened. This idea constitutes the ground for the causality-as-process-tracing approach we present in this chapter. Causal process and causal interaction are the two main concepts in Salmon's approach. A causal process refers to the direct link connecting a cause and an effect, through which a mark is transmitted that modifies the process of how something evolves. A process is causal if it is capable of transmitting the modification of its structure that occurs in a single local interaction. It has been argued that a world characterized by transmissions of causal influences and propensities to interact is closer to the Weberian conception of social science than to the Hempelian deductive monarchy (Mantzavinos 2018). This idea, we believe, is a good starting point for transforming questions obsessively focused on describing lived experiences (what is the lived experience of growing old, of being solitary, of being unemployed and so forth), which abound in qualitative research into causal questions, enabling comparison and causal thinking as a means of crafting explanatory propositions. For example, a causal question could be what are the causes of choosing internet dating by middle-aged people or why university students drop out of their studies; or even why certain groups of unemployed experience unemployment in differentiated ways. For Mahoney (2012), to the extent that one puts centre-stage the question "Was X a cause of Y in case Z?", process tracing can be used as a method for evaluating hypotheses about the causes of a specific outcome in a particular case.

Mahoney (2012) thinks that two criteria must be satisfied for the identification of causal processes: first, that specific unobserved events or processes take place; second, that there is a causal connection between two or more events or processes. The first criterion involves a descriptive inference about what actually happened in the history of a given case, while the second seeks to establish causality among events or processes that are believed to have occurred within a given case. Note that these criteria express a realist view according to which social facts exist independently of the observer and can be known through causal inferences. What is identified is not only whether a given hypothesis is valid but also whether contradictory alternatives are not valid.

The process tracing approach to causal explanation is in line with the call for micro-foundations demanded by Little, but it conceives of mechanisms in an ontological rather than an instrumental way. Instead of treating causal mechanisms as "analytical constructs", process tracing theorists prefer to accept Bhaskar's realist approach to causal explanation, which we analyzed in the previous chapter. Indeed, Mahoney defines social mechanisms as unobservable entities that, when activated, generate an outcome of interest. George and Bennett provide a more comprehensive definition of causal mechanisms as

> ultimately unobservable physical, social or psychological processes through which agents with causal capacities operate, but only in specific contexts or conditions, to transfer energy, information or matter to other entities. In so doing, the causal agent changes the affected entities' characteristics capacities or propensities in ways that persist until subsequent causal mechanisms act upon it.
>
> (George and Bennett 2005, 137)

This definition puts at the forefront three things: first, the contextual nature of a mechanism-based explanation; second, the fact that a mechanism is a difference-making process; and, third, that mechanisms are conceived in a counterfactual manner.[1] George and Bennett underline the fact that their definition is the opposite of definitions that emphasize the predictive capacities of constant conjunctions and that make use of regression models based on a regularity conception of causality proposed by Humean philosophies. We believe that George and Bennett's definition fits more with qualitative methodologies because it encourages social scientists to forge causal hypotheses when they try to make sense of the amount of data they have gathered. We should stress that George and Bennett do not favour reductionism because they do not identify micro-foundations with observable individual-level properties. On the contrary, given that mechanisms remain at the unobservable level, they can be tapped at the irreducible level of the social (for example, relations, groups and institutions). In other words, whereas individualists presuppose social entities in their conceptions of causality but deny attributing causal power to them, process tracing theorists accept the causal efficacy of unobservable social entities. This is the difference between seeing causal mechanisms as an epistemological concept and seeing them as an ontological one.

Bennett and Checkel also avoid viewing these processes as "intervening variables", preferring to define them as "sequences, and conjunctures of events within a case for the purposes of either developing or testing hypotheses about causal mechanisms that might causally explain the case" (Bennett and Checkel 2015, 8). The mechanism-based approach to causality provides us with the means for tapping the process through which a phenomenon/event is generated by referring to the relations formed by its constituents. Of course, this is at odds with the exceptionless conception of causality proposed by the deductive-nomological (D-N) model. In other words, mechanism-based explanations describe how parts interact in such a way that a phenomenon takes place. These explanations are not a threat to sociology because the explanatory potential of generative mechanisms is deployed at the configurational rather than the individual level.

Things become complicated and intriguing when theoretical attention is paid to the "case", defined as the "instantiation of a class of events". Given that qualitative researchers' raw material comprises "cases", it follows that a crucial issue concerns the answer to the question "What is a case?", most successfully developed in Ragin and Becker's classic book (1992). What we believe is the cornerstone of their book is that qualitative researchers should make sense of the social world by means of asking the following question: "What phenomenon is this instance a case of?" In other words, the key to causal thinking is what Ragin (1992) calls "casing". Casing can be seen as a way of relating the singular with the universal when one tries to connect research data with the case for which these data have been gathered and with the phenomenon of which this case is an instance. The fact that qualitative researchers deal with the singular does not mean that they are preoccupied with the particularity of an inexplicable thing or with ungraspable peculiarities for which the only thing that can be done is to describe its uniqueness (the so-called "idiographic approach"). On the contrary, the singular is not an empirical matter as positivists conceive of it in a nominalistic way, because it always tells us something about the objects of which it is an instantiation. It has, in other words, an illustrative value in so far as it elucidates the whole by detailing its social formation. Casing, in addition, may lead to causal hypotheses that shed light on the conditions that increase the probability of specific things happening. For Ragin, cases are meaningful configurations and wholes of events and structures that are selected not by observing isolated singulars but by identifying phenomena in similar settings, for purposes of comparison and contrast. In this sense, cases are not fully delineated at the start of the research process but rather are gradually crystallized while the interaction between theory and data gathering is in process. The *raison d'être* of casing is to make comparisons through which new hypotheses might arise. For example, a researcher examining habitus formation in working-class adolescents residing in two neighbourhoods that differ in terms of social background might not only compare these two groups of working-class adolescents, but also contrast working-class adolescents who choose to attend general senior high-school after junior high school with working-class adolescents who choose to attend vocational school after junior high school. The goals of casing are concept formation and theory development or refinement, rather than merely to verify or falsify a deductively created hypothesis. As the boundaries of cases shift, concepts are clarified and revised. Through casing, one can identify causal mechanisms and the necessary and sufficient conditions in which they are enacted.

That casing enables researchers to bring to light causal mechanisms which are embedded in necessary and sufficient conditions constitutes an issue that has been misunderstood the most by those who tend to make sense of qualitative research through the statistical inferential logic. In order to rectify this misunderstanding, we think that it is useful to reformulate with sociology examples of the difference between necessary and sufficient conditions, as analyzed by Goertz and Mahoney (2012). Necessary conditions can be formulated as follows:

[1] X is necessary for Y = Y is a subset of X

Proposition [1] can be depicted as a Venn diagram as follows:

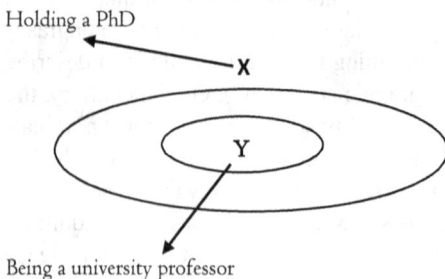

Figure 4.1 Something is necessary.

By contrast, sufficient conditions can be formulated as follows:

[2] X is sufficient for Y = X is a subset of Y

Proposition [2] can be depicted as a Venn diagram as follows:

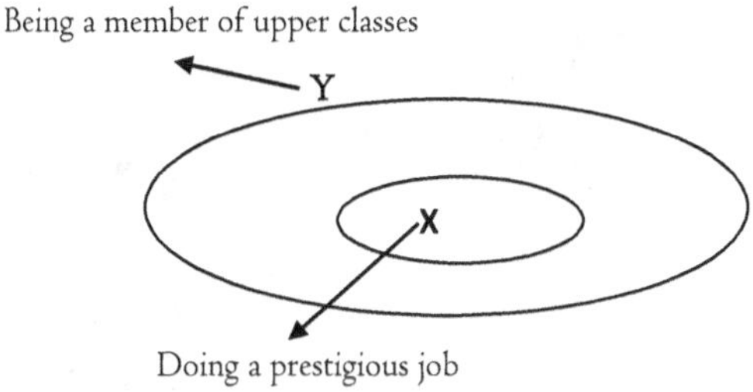

Being a member of upper classes

Doing a prestigious job

Figure 4.2 Something is sufficient.

Necessary conditions of proposition [1] can be depicted in the following 2X2 table

Table 4.1 Combinations of necessary conditions

		X	
		0	**1**
Y	**1**	0	N
	0	N	N

while sufficient conditions of proposition [2] can be depicted in the following 2X2 table

Table 4.2 Combinations of sufficient conditions

		X	
		0	**1**
Y	**1**	N	N
	0	N	0

Table 4.1 presents the possible combinations between X and Y, with the 0 within the cell denoting that the combination that "not having a PhD and being a university professor" is impossible. The values 0 and 1 denote whether being or having X or Y apply or not. In this sense, the combinations

"not holding a PhD and not being a university professor",
"holding a PhD and being a university professor" and
"holding a PhD and not being a university professor" can be possible.

In the same way, in Table 4.2 the combination "doing a prestigious job and not being a member of the upper classes" is impossible, whereas the combinations:

"not doing a prestigious job and being a member of the middle classes",
"not doing a prestigious job and not being a member of the middle classes"
"doing a prestigious job and being a member of the middle classes" can be
   possible.

As one can easily see, the difference lies in the fact that the ways in which the entities of the social world are related can be conceived by means of either the statistical logic or the set-theoretic logic. Quantitative researchers tend to believe that it is only the statistical inference that matters and thereby confuse necessary with sufficient conditions. One of the consequences of this confusion is that most of the time quantitative researchers end up stating the obvious because of the difference between stating that "all X are Y" and "all Y are X". Holding a PhD is necessary for being a university professor, but X is not sufficient for Y as there are lots of people who hold a PhD but are not university professors. In other words, when statisticians say that "all X are Y", it is not clear whether they mean that Y is a subset of X or vice versa. Instead they are trying to specify probabilistically how much of X affects Y by using mean average effect measures.

   It is upon this misunderstanding that the confounding of causes-of-effects with effects-of-causes rests. The difference is rooted in whether one starts from the outcome or from the causes. Quantitative scholars, by posing effects-of-causes types of questions, focus on estimating the average effects of particular variables in a population, while case-oriented researchers favour explanations of outcomes and the effects of particular causal mechanisms within cases. The aim of case-oriented researchers is to develop causes-of-effects models by identifying combinations of conditions, including the non-trivial necessary and sufficient. Instead of focusing on "independent" and "control" variables in order that a statistician can deal with the problem of equifinality, process tracing theorists are in favour of identifying the causal field that makes something happen. This explains why quantitative scholars translate differently from qualitative researchers the question "What causes Y?" Whereas quantitative scholars read the question as "What is the average effect of X on Y in a population of cases?", qualitative researchers prefer to read it as "What Xs explain Y for one or more specific cases?" By identifying "A causes B" with "the effect of A is B", statisticians emphasize only the average effects of particular independent variables on the phenomenon of interest, while, on the contrary, case researchers prioritize the development of causal arguments intended to specify the factors that are jointly sufficient for the outcome and that explain the specific case.

The above remarks encapsulate why it is not by accident that the process tracing approaches to causality and to casing are very close to the INUS theory of causality proposed by Mackie.[2] As is well-known, Mackie's example is about how one can identify the causes of a fire that has broken out in a house. The cause proposed by the experts (an electrical short-circuit in a certain place) is not for Mackie a necessary condition, because the fire might have occurred through the overturning of a lighted oil stove or through a number of other things. In the same way, it is not a sufficient condition because even if the short-circuit had occurred but there had been no inflammable material nearby, then the fire would not have broken out and even if both the short-circuit and the inflammable material were true, the fire would not have occurred had, say, there been an efficient automatic sprinkler in the right spot. Instead of treating an electrical short-circuit as either a necessary or a sufficient condition, Mackie prefers to see it as an indispensable part of a complex condition. According to this approach, the cause is an insufficient but necessary part of a condition which is itself unnecessary but sufficient for the result (INUS causal field). Let us clarify Mackie's argument by presenting an example from the field of sociology of education.

Habitus dislocation is a term used to denote the clash and the disjunction that an agent experiences when he or she faces a context or a situation in which the habitus demanded exists in an opposite direction to his or her past habitus. Emotional distress or the sense that one is seen as "the fly in the glass" is the main lived experience of habitus dislocation. The two most studied areas of habitus dislocation are geographical mobility (for educational purposes or migration) and educational mobility. As far as the latter is concerned, habitus dislocation concerns the gulf between the habitus of those from a working-class milieu and the middle-class habitus demanded by the university culture in which they come to live. The question is whether working-class background constitutes a sufficient condition for habitus dislocation and whether working-class students experience it in a similar manner. Social scientists who transfer deductive thinking into social matters would answer in the affirmative since they approach causes through the language of variables of the type "if A, then B" and identify the "cause" of the outcome (habitus dislocation) with the working-class background. By contrast, Mackie's argument invites us to think in terms of the following figure:

```
┌─────────────────────────┐
│ A    B    C    D    E    │─────────▶  OUTCOME (TYPES OF HABITUS
└──────────────┬──────────┘                      DISLOCATION)
               │
               ▼
```

CONDITION X= UNNECESSARY BUT SUFFICIENT

A = Rupture with parents' life plans
B = Family's strategy for the entry of its offspring into the university
C = Conflictual social relationships with individuals coming from the milieu of class origin
D = Adopting the university language codes and culture
E = Starting a romantic affair with a person of middle-class culture

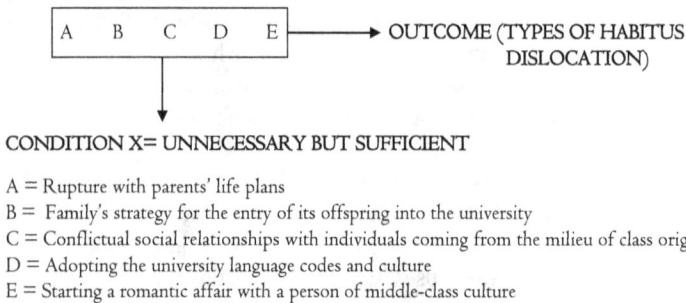

Figure 4.3 A sociological example of INUS condition.

Given that A, B, C, D and E are contingent and do not denote a hierarchy in any sense, the question remains which configuration of these five parts is the "necessary but insufficient" part of the unnecessary but sufficient condition X that causes a peculiar type of habitus dislocation to occur. In our view and in relation to the above example, the importance of thinking in INUS terms is that it enables us to refine the concept of habitus dislocation and to identify that upwardly mobile university students may develop either an either/or habitus dislocation type or a both/and type (Christodoulou and Spyridakis 2016). In the first case, dislocation is not experienced in disruptive terms in the sense that agents can easily reconcile their past and present habitus, while the second type of dislocation is more disjunctive because agents are trying to get rid of their past habitus. The rationale of this methodological reasoning is to deny the crude and variable-oriented idea that social mobility through education causes habitus dislocation while bringing to light the necessary and sufficient conditions within which specific social mechanisms cause specific types of habitus dislocation to occur. There is no reason to expand more on this issue. What interests us is that qualitative researchers can identify minimal sufficient conditions and their combinations that cause something to occur. Is this a causal explanation in Mackie's terms? Yes: and it is here that one can find one of the main subtle but crucial differences between the variable-oriented and the case-oriented researcher.

Variable-oriented researchers, by identifying an explanation through "explaining variation", would compare samples taken from the independent variable (students of middle-class origin versus upwardly mobile working-class students) and would conclude that the cause is the class origin. By contrast, for case-oriented researchers, what matters is the identification of the causal path leading from X (a specific class situation) to Y (habitus dislocation). What needs to be stressed is that even though the phenomenon "habitus dislocation" can be researched in such varied fields as migration, turning points or unemployment, the way this phenomenon is instantiated in the field of educational mobility has been gradually constituted through dialogue between data and theoretical ideas developed during the research process. Whereas for variable-oriented researchers the population is a taken-for-granted issue, case-oriented researchers consider the selection of cases as a theory-laden process in need of careful examination. In our example, if case studies of instances of "the upwardly mobile working-class students" are accumulated, then the causal field consists of A, B, C, D, E, and their possible combinations can be identified as one of several configurations for habitus dislocation. This is the reason why the process tracing explanation framed by the INUS condition is deemed to provide the ground for a unifying theory of causality.

The strength of the process tracing approach to causality is that it enables us to identify in detail the various combinations of causes through which similar outcomes in different settings are produced (conjunctural causation, or causal heterogeneity) and not the relative strength of each variable. Instead of bivariate correlations, case-oriented researchers emphasize causal conjunctures because the magnitude of any single cause's impact depends upon the presence or absence of other causal conditions. This is the reason why such researchers can refine or develop theory more satisfactorily than those who insist on approaching the social world through regression statistical models. An additional strength of the process tracing approach concerns the tools it offers for eliminating alternative explanations. For that goal, case-oriented researchers dispute the probabilistic conception of causality according to which the values of a variable are considered the causes of an outcome. Simply stated, this means that it is the specific values of a variable that raise the probability of an outcome happening. In our view, two questionable assumptions sustain this probability-raiser conception of explanation: first, that the probability is a property of the population; and second, that the values that raise the probability of the outcome to the population have the power to raise the probability of the same outcome to happen in the singular case (and given that deductive thinking is reductionist when applied in the social world, it follows that in this way of thinking the singular case is identified with the individual).

Mahoney (2008) raises the objection that variable-oriented researchers cannot handle cases where the so-called cause is absent but the outcome takes place. Contrarily, case-oriented research is able to overcome a) the difficulty of whether X causes Y or vice versa and b) the spuriousness related to whether there is some intervening variable between X and Y, as it is the details of the process that are highlighted in the identification of the causal path. George and Bennett (2005) hold that cases provide us with evidence that can affirm one explanation and/or disconfirm others, while at the same time numerous other pieces of evidence may not be covered among the explanations at all. What matters is not the amount of evidence, but its contribution to adjudicating among alternative hypotheses.

From the above it follows that mechanisms can be defined generally as unobserved factors that lie between an explanatory variable and an outcome in a causal chain. Neil Gross (2018) has pointed out that the structure of these chains can present four kinds of variations. First, they may compile a few mechanisms or they may be composed of many mechanisms. The fact that sometimes the causal chains contain too many mechanisms means that the more complex the configuration of mechanisms the more the number of conditionals triggering them and, as a consequence, the harder it is to theorize upon them and the greater the chance of error. For this reason, social scientists should be very attentive to the explanatory power of mechanisms in such cases. Second, causal chains differ as to the issue of over how long a period of time the chain unfolds. Third, causal chains may be deployed in a vertical ontological level or alternatively be identified across the same ontological level. In the first case the unit of analysis may be an institution or an organization, while in the second the unit of analysis may comprise various kinds of actors (identity formation or networks). Finally, causal chains vary in the abstract patterns formed by connections among mechanisms: in the nature of the flow across them.

Process tracing theorists take INUS causes to be the missing link for settling the ground for a unified conception of causality. For them, INUS causes are treated as probability raisers or as probabilistically necessary factors that usually or almost always have to be present for the outcome to occur. They are thus normally present in the different combinations of causes that can each generate the outcome of interest. Additionally, there are important INUS causes that do not have to be combined with many other conditions to generate the outcome of interest, they are probabilistically sufficient. The goal is to identify the causal links between X1 (explanatory condition) and Y (outcome) across settings, not just how an outcome emerges in a particular setting. However, Mahoney (2008) underlines the fact that one should not take as causes the individual variables connected with the partial effects shown in the statistical models. It is not the statistical coefficient that makes them causes but rather the fact that they are important INUS causes (i.e. they are probabilistically necessary and/or sufficient for outcomes to occur). Case selection and sampling are the key to achieving these goals and in chapter 5 we will say more on this issue. For now it suffices to note that case-oriented researchers believe that cases have a lot to contribute as far as theory development is concerned. Their contribution centres on three areas:

- First, on establishing, strengthening or weakening an already known theory;
- Second, finding that a theory explains or not a case may be generalizable to the type or class of cases of which this case is a member;
- Third, case study findings may be generalizable to the role played by a process in dissimilar cases.

Deviant cases are crucial for theory development because they do not fit researchers' evolving schemes or are not explained by some existing theory. For George and Bennett (2005), theory development has much to gain from the analysis of negative cases for identifying new dimensions in a causal mechanism. As we tried to show with the habitus dislocation example above, negative cases' merit is the reformulation of some of the hypotheses stemming from Bourdieu's theory regarding the causes of this phenomenon and the development of new dimensions regarding his theory on cleft habitus. As to the generalizability issue, this refinement may lead to contingent generalizations by constructing a new type of the phenomenon. It is perplexing when one says that case-oriented researchers generalize not in relation to the particulars (that is, to a population of individuals) but to a set of events of which a unique case is an instantiation. This means that a unique case may be an instantiation of, say, identity change, decision making for postgraduate studies. This is what qualitative researchers mean when they say that generalization concerns processes, not populations. The key once again is casing and to think in set-theoretic terms. In this way, one is able to generalize about how the newly identified causal mechanism plays out in different contexts, to test and delineate the scope conditions in which a theory applies and to eliminate alternative explanations.

We believe that these are some of the distinguishing features for thinking causally when practising qualitative or in particular biographical research and they should not be confused with some of the logical-empiricist assumptions of the quantitative tradition. As Maxwell (2004; 2012) and Abbott (1988; 2016) have repeatedly argued, many aspects of social phenomena cannot be subsumed under the linear regression model, which is implemented to estimate the $\beta 1$ effect of $X1$ on Y and to eliminate the $\gamma 1$ effect of $C1$ on Y. This model is an expression of Mill's classic methods of agreement and difference. Let us briefly clarify in a simple example how these methods work. Regarding the method of agreement, suppose that one is researching the causes of the phenomenon (F) of "the transition from postgraduate to PhD studies" and that one proposes that three causes of F are: a) obtaining qualifications for successful job market prospects (C1); b) pursuing an academic career (C2); and c) self-realization (C3). The researcher then selects the case of "School of Social Sciences" (Case 1) and finds that all three causes exist. The method of agreement proceeds by elimination. The researcher tries to find other cases – for example, the "School of Polytechnics" (Case 2) or the "School of Medicine" (Case 3) – for which one of the causes does not exist in order to eliminate it as a cause. When the researcher finds cases in which causes are not absent that cannot be eliminated, he/she has identified the cause(s) of the phenomenon. This is a classic procedure of looking for invariance patterns in the sense that the researcher is searching for variables that appear regularly through all the cases. However, the method of agreement suffers from two inadequacies. First, only sufficient and not necessary relations are identified, because the relation between C1 and Case 1 may be mediated by a possible fourth cause (C4). Second, the issue of multiple causation cannot be overcome: there are cases in which only C1 exists and cases in which only C2 exists. In the method of difference, researchers look for cases in which the presence of C1 is followed by the presence of F and for cases in which the absence of C1 is followed by the absence of F. Then, a 2X2 table is produced, where C1 is the cause of F if and only if all the studied cases fall under the cell of presence/presence and of absence/absence.

Instead of this correlational concept of causation, case researchers implement set-theoretic ideas so that combinations of interconnected factors constitute efficient causal conditions making something happen.[3] Goertz and Mahoney (2012) have shown how this combinatory field of interacting causes can be depicted in a formal way through the symbols of logic and set theory. The idea proposed has two parts: first, one has to identify the sufficient causal set conditions that make something happen; second, by identifying the set where these conditions intersect, one has identified the necessary conditions of the phenomenon of interest. In other words, membership in each of these sufficient set conditions is necessary for something to happen.

Ragin (2008) explains this idea by stating that there are two ways through which one can identify commonalities across a set of cases. The first is to research cases sharing a given outcome and then to identify their shared causal (necessary) conditions; the second is to research cases sharing a specific causal condition and then to examine whether these cases are sufficient for exhibiting the same outcome. In the first way, the instances of the outcome are a subset of the instances of the causal conditions and in the second way the instances of the causal conditions are a subset of the instances of an outcome. These are two strategies for establishing explicit connections across cases. What Ragin tries to say is that set-theoretic connections are completely at odds with correlational methods of agreement and difference, the reason being that the former are asymmetrical while the latter are symmetrical. For example, in following a set-theoretic connection, one can state that unemployed people are vulnerable without this being challenged by the fact that there are vulnerable people who are not unemployed. What this statement says is simply that unemployed people are a subset of vulnerable people. What those who apply variable-oriented thinking to qualitative research miss is that they conflate the distinction between symmetrical and asymmetrical connections. Following Ragin, we illustrate this point by cross-tabulating in a 2x2 table the presence/absence of an outcome (vulnerability) against the presence/absence of a hypothesized cause (unemployment) (Table 4.3).

Table 4.3 An example of presence/absence of outcome and cause

	Causal condition absent (unemployment)	Causal condition present (unemployment)
Outcome present (vulnerability)	[1] Cases undermining the researcher's argument that "unemployment causes vulnerability"	[2] Cases supporting the researcher's argument that "unemployment causes vulnerability"
Outcome absent (vulnerability)	[3] Cases supporting the researcher's argument that "unemployment causes vulnerability"	[4] Cases undermining the researcher's argument that "unemployment causes vulnerability"

If one reads this table through a correlational line of reasoning, he/she looks both at cells [2] and [3] in order to confirm his/her hypotheses that "unemployment causes vulnerability" and at cells [1] and [4] because they confirm the hypotheses through a counterfactual way. By contrast, a set-theoretic line of reasoning interested in causal conditions shared by instances of an outcome would focus on cells [1] and [2], while a set-theoretic line of reasoning interested in whether cases that are similar with respect to causal conditions experience the same outcome would focus on cells [2] and [4]. Ragin underlines the fact that researchers are called to solve a paradox: why two different conditions ([2] and [4]) lead to the same outcome. Is there a common element that explains it? The same paradox holds for cases sharing the same causal condition but leading to different outcomes ([1] and [3]). Here the goal is to identify the difference responsible for these contradictory outcomes. We can illustrate Ragin's paradox through an interview-based study. Spyridakis (2018) has searched for causal links between unemployment and vulnerability and has stated that "long-term unemployed people who have neither social ties nor state-funded or other sources are vulnerable". One may reformulate this causal connection by saying that "being long-term unemployed with no social ties and with no state-funded or other sources" is a sufficient condition for being vulnerable. In set-theoretic terms this can be visualized as follows:

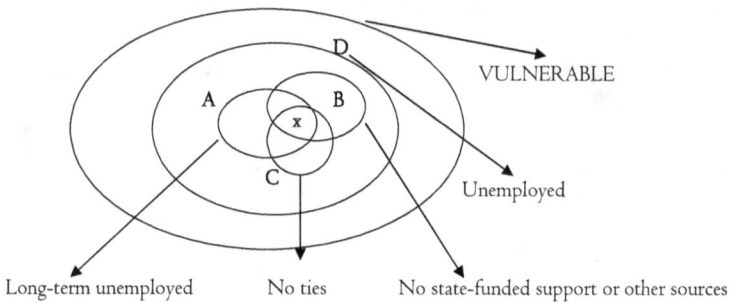

Figure 4.4 Presenting causal connections in set-theoretic terms. An example.

This figure can be stated in formal terms as follows: A ∩ B ∩ C subset D subset Vulnerability.

In other words, the point x is where A, B and C intersect and this is a subset of unemployed people or, stated more clearly, the "long-term unemployed with no social ties and with no state-funded or other sources" is a subset of the set "vulnerable people". Ragin thinks that the most serious mistake made by those who apply quantitative reasoning to qualitative research is the transformation of qualitative data into nominal variables that are added in a numerical manner. By contrast, Ragin believes that one can address the degree of membership in sets by using values in the interval between 0.0 (non-membership) and 1.0 (full membership). In this way, sets are treated as continuous (interval or ratio) variables but through a clearly qualitative lens, enabling one to detect causal connections between social phenomena that can be strong, no matter how weak they may be through correlational thinking.

Given that sufficient causation exists when X is a subset of Y, Ragin defines a subset relation when the membership scores in one set (e.g. a causal condition or a combination of causal conditions) are consistently less than or equal to their corresponding membership scores in another set (e.g. the outcome). Thus, in our example, the above statement can be transformed as follows: "among the unemployed, the long-term employed and those who lack social ties and other sources are the most vulnerable". Recalling what we said before on process tracing, this is a causal hypothesis that identifies the causal link connecting unemployment with vulnerability. This is an asymmetrical hypothesis because it does not state that there exists no unemployed who are not vulnerable, but explains a within-case causal path. It is obvious that if one wants to sidestep the possibility that this causal hypothesis is merely a coincidence, he/she should follow a simple proportional thought: the more cases exhibiting the cause or the combination of causes as well as the outcome, the more consistent the causal connection.

The merit of such causal thinking is that it enables one to detect the specifics of causal configurations as highlighted by the researcher, rather than to measure the effect of an independent variable on the dependent. In this sense, in the above example vulnerability in relation to long-term unemployment matters when it is combined with the presence of both no ties and no resources and gives us a clue why social science researchers have to be clear about the scope conditions to which the causal hypothesis applies. It is the membership in the intersection point x that is sufficient for vulnerability. It is through set-theoretic reasoning that one can bring to light the causal path leading to a particular outcome explaining why case process tracing researchers prefer causal configuration to "statistical interaction" measures as the best way to overcome equifinality (different causes produce the same outcome). It is important to note that the comparative logic such as that proposed by Ragin aims to strengthen one's confidence that a theory can be both causally explanatory and to overcome the impasses of equifinality stemming from Mill's method of agreement and difference. This is why case-oriented researchers have made use of Mackie's INUS condition and set theory. Furthermore, this is why they prioritize the identification of a causal chain leading from causal conditions to the outcome as a way to detect spuriousness, causal priority (whether the causal condition is necessary for the outcome) and causal depth (how much explanatory power the causal condition has). In the next chapter we show how one can combine the process tracing approach to causality with what scholars of reconstructive biographical research (RBR) say about the relation between the singular and the universal.

Notes

1 This definition of social mechanisms is in line with Gorskis' definition (2009, 163) of social mechanisms being "emergent causal powers of related entities within a system", where "related entities" are approached as "entities and relationships that are necessary to the recurring effects of the mechanism in question".

2 According to Mackie, "the so-called cause is, and is known to be, an insufficient but necessary part of a condition which is itself unnecessary but sufficient for the result" (Mackie 1965, 245).

3 We firmly believe that the set-theoretic fuzzy reasoning of process tracing theorists is compatible with the concept of relational feedback proposed by critical realists. One of its core theoretical assumptions is that relational logic is a
combinatory logic based upon interaction and contradictory complementarity
between opposite realities that accepts the paradoxes as a matter of fact, rather
than excluding them as "illogical". It is by virtue of the relational character of
the reality that two opposite representations of the same reality can coexist *at
the same time*. As Donati (2015, 79) notes, "[a] feedback can maintain a sort of
complementarity between its negative and positive dimensions ('I accept and do
not accept at the same time', referring of course to different objects: I accept the
relationship but not the proposed solution). This apparently leads to paradoxes,
and, in fact, one speaks of fuzzy logic or logic of paradoxes. This principle
refers to all cases where oppositions belong together as complementary without
forming a whole".

References

Abbott, A. "Transcending General Linear Reality." *Sociological Theory* 6, no. 2
   (1988): 169–86.
Abbott, A. *Processual Sociology*. Chicago and London: The University of Chicago
   Press, 2016.
Bennett, A., and J.T. Checkel. "Process Tracing: From Philosophical Roots to Best
   Practices." In *Process Tracing: From Metaphor to Analytic Tool*, edited by
   A. Bennett, and J.T. Checkel, 3–38. Cambridge: Cambridge University Press,
   2015.
Christodoulou, M., and M. Spyridakis. "Upwardly Mobile Working-Class
   Adolescents: A Biographical Approach on Habitus Dislocation." *Cambridge
   Journal of Education* 47, no. 3 (2016): 315–35.
Donati, P. "Social Mechanisms and Their Feedbacks: Mechanical vs Relational
   Emergence of New Social Formations." In *Generative Mechanisms Transforming
   the Social Order*, edited by M. Archer, 65–95. New York: Springer, 2015.
George, L.A., and A. Bennett. *Case Studies and Theory Development in the Social
   Sciences*. Massachusetts: MIT Press, 2005.
Goertz, G., and J. Mahoney. *A Tale of Two Cultures. Qualitative and Quantitative
   Research in the Social Sciences*. Princeton and Oxford: Princeton University
   Press, 2012.
Gorski, P. "Social "Mechanisms" and Comparative-Historical Sociology: A Critical
   Realist Proposal." In *Frontiers of Sociology*, edited by P. Hedström, and B.
   Wittrock, 147–94. Leiden/Boston: Brill, 2009.
Gross, N. "The Structure of Causal Chains." *Sociological Theory* 36, no. 4 (2018):
   1–25. doi:10.1177/0735275118811377.
Mackie, J. "Causes and Conditions." *American Philosophical Quarterly* 2, no. 4
   (1965): 245–64.
Mahoney, J. "Toward a Unified Theory of Causality." *Comparative Political Studies*
   41, no. 4–5 (2008): 412–36. doi:10.1177/0010414007313115.

Mahoney, J. "The Logic of Process Tracing Tests in the Social Sciences." *Sociological Methods & Research* 41, no. 4 (2012): 1–28. doi:10.1177/0049124 112437709.

Mantzavinos, C. *A Dialogue on Explanation.* Heidelberg and New York: Springer, 2018.

Maxwell, A.J. "Causal Explanation, Qualitative Research and Scientific Inquiry in Education." *Educational Researcher* 33, no. 2 (2004): 3–11. doi:10.3102/0013189X033002003.

Maxwell, A.J. *A Realist Approach for Qualitative Research.* London: Sage Publications, 2012.

Ragin, C.C. "Introduction: Cases of 'What Is a Case?'" In *What Is a Case? Exploring the Foundations of Social Inquiry,* edited by C.C. Ragin, and H.S. Becker, 1–20. Cambridge: Cambridge University Press, 1992.

Ragin, C.C. *Redesigning Social Inquiry. Fuzzy Sets and Beyond.* Chicago and London: University of Chicago Press, 2008.

Ragin, C.C., and H.S. Becker. *What Is a Case? Exploring the Foundations of Social Inquiry.* Cambridge: Cambridge University Press, 1992.

Spyridakis, M. *Homo Precarious. Experiencing Vulnerability During Crisis.* Athens: Pedio (in Greek), 2018.

5 Relating cases with phenomena
Arguments for generalizing through mechanisms

One of the main thrusts of this book is that cases constitute a powerful tool for identifying the generative mechanisms explaining why something happens and that reconstructive biographical research (RBR), by treating research material (life stories) in a holistic way, has much to contribute to this goal. As Apitsch and Inowlocki (2000) highlight, the focus of RBR is not the reconstruction of intentionality that is represented as an individual's life course, but the embeddedness of the biographical account in social macro-structures. The general assumption of the reconstructive tradition is that it is possible to trace or reconstruct general statements or general traces of social phenomena in a single case study. Methodologically, this means that a single case study has to be researched in its "wholeness" in order to reconstruct the intermingling of agency and social structures (Siouti 2017). Those who dispute such a claim believe that the main deficiency of case studies is their inadequacy to generalize. In this way, they put at the forefront the issue of how the singular is related to the general. However, it has been shown that such a reservation is based on a Humean conception of causality that tends to identify causation with constant conjunction and makes sense of generalization in numerical terms. By contrast, here we provide arguments that dispute the notion that generalization is dependent on the frequency of occurrence (Rosenthal 2018). In this chapter we argue in favour of alternative ways of approaching generalizability as well as of RBR scholars' perspective towards the transition from the singular to the general. In addition, we show how generalizing through case studies is tied up with explaining causally the social.

According to Small (2009), to the extent that they investigate a limited number of cases, qualitative researchers and in particular ethnographers are pressured by various evaluation or funding committees to prove that their findings are generalizable. Some come to adopt most of the nominalist assumptions of quantitative researchers in order to circumvent this pressure by applying quantitative criteria of sampling (like the concept of "representativeness") to their object construction. However, to Small, this practice is hardly appropriate for qualitative research given the contextual, contingent and complex aspects of most social phenomena. Even if researchers try to implement the logic of representativeness and randomization, they are likely to fail for two reasons. The first has to do with the fact that cases selected will always be considered "biased" because sampling in qualitative research is purposive. The second reason is that qualitative researchers, by using this kind of sampling, will never be able to prove whether their analyses concerning their sampling units would be the same if they had been applied to the entire population. Thus, instead of mimicking the logical-empiricist assumptions of quantitative research, social researchers would have to think of alternative ways to approach the relation of the case to the phenomenon of interest. Let us briefly reconstruct Small's comments on the alternatives offered by Burawoy's "extended case method" (Burawoy 1998; Burawoy et al. 1991) and Mitchell's "extended case study" (1983).

The term "extended" in Burawoy's conception seems to answer how the theoretical or conceptual formulations obtained from the analysis of a case may be extended to other groups or aggregations, to other bounded contexts or places, or to other sociocultural domains. However, a closer look at this argument reveals that Burawoy is not highlighting the singular causes of a case and is not answering how his findings may extend or be transferred to other contexts. He examines the case to ascertain how larger forces shape the conditions: "the analyst investigates society at large to determine its impacts on the case at hand" (Small 2009, 20). In this way, the importance of the single case lies in what it tells us about society as a whole rather than about the population of similar cases (Burawoy et al. 1991). While Burawoy's ideas seem to provide an alternative approach to the case-phenomenon relation, by trying to identify social influences, he sets in motion a deductive line of reasoning that forces data. Burawoy's analysis of a case is not oriented towards theory development even though in his later writings (1998) he acknowledges that case studies and deviant cases may contribute to refining or reconstructing existing theory.

Before Burawoy, Glyde Mitchell (1983) was the first to extensively discuss the merits of studying cases in order to identify the processes connecting seemingly unrelated events that evolve over time: "The extended case study enables the analyst to trace how events chain on to one another and how therefore events are necessarily linked to one another through time" (Mitchell 1983, 194). As Small (2009) notes, for Mitchell what is at stake is not explaining local conditions in light of external forces, but showing how cases contribute to uncovering mechanisms and tracing processes. Mitchell goes even further by stating that the appropriate procedures for making inferences from statistical data are quite different from those implemented to study the combination of elements or events that constitute a "case". In contrast to statistical inference procedures based on representativeness, in case analysis "extrapolation is in fact based on the validity of the analysis rather than the representativeness of the events" (Mitchell 1983, 190). In this way, the inference is "logical" or "causal" and concerns "the process by which the analyst draws conclusions about the essential linkage between two or more characteristics in terms of some explanatory schema" (Mitchell 1983, 200).

Following Mitchell's ideas, Small (2009) holds that researchers should aim to craft causal hypotheses based on "logical" or "causal" inferences that are appropriate for uncovering mechanisms and tracing processes. He shows why "statistical inference" is doomed to fail by providing various examples. For instance, observing that most of the teachers in an elementary school are women does not tell us that educationalists in most of the elementary schools in the country are women: only if the social mechanism sustaining this correlation is identified may one hold this generalization. For instance, by analyzing the case, one may identify that women choose this job to harmonize family and work demands. Hypothesizing that such a finding can be transferred to similar contexts is not based on a statistical but on a "logical" or "causal" inference. Two points can be added that are close to Small's argument: a) this kind of generalizing is similar to Cronbach's (1975, 125) idea that "generalization is a working hypothesis, not a conclusion"; and b) representativeness is not to be identified with the sample-population relation but concerns the extent to which a causal hypothesis emerges from cases covering most of the various and divergent aspects of the phenomenon.

Small's approach resembles how RBR scholars view the case-phenomenon relation. Given that RBR is not limited to an ideographic description of an individual case, RBR scholars hold that the Weberian-inspired way of typological theorizing is a fruitful solution. What needs to be stressed, however, is that for RBR, "typical" does not mean "representativeness" but rather revolves around the following line of reasoning. RBR treats the general not in numerical terms but in a dialectical way, in which the general can be found in the individual. Each individual case is constituted within a social reality and can reveal something about the relationship between the individual and the general. It emerges from the general and is a particular exemplar of the general. Thus, each individual case can tell us something about the general in its specific instantiation in relation to specific conditions (Rosenthal 2018). In order to trace how each individual case instantiates the phenomenon of interest, researchers must decode the constitutive moments of the phenomenon as it takes shape in a specific case. It is here that generalization and explanation meet and culminate in the concept of "typical" in the following sense: explanation is to reconstruct those complex processes connecting two separate and changing events and to bring to light the configuration of the causal chain that connects them. Explaining a social phenomenon is to identify its colligation with other events and to highlight the inherent relations sustaining it within specific historical conditions (Przyborsky and Wohlrab-Sahr 2010). Following Mayntz (2002), Przyborsky and Wohlrab-Sahr (2010) propose the term "causal reconstruction" to underline how what is generalizable is not social laws but peculiar mechanisms that connect causes with outcomes.[1] This approach to generalizing presupposes the following steps. First, the rules that generate a case and organize its manifold parts are reconstructed. In this way, the typicality of a case is brought to light that constitutes the organizing structure of the case as it has been crystallized through time. Second, researchers leave the level of analyzing an individual case and move to comparing contrastively various cases not by focusing on their demographic properties but on their structural similarities and differences.

The causal propositions or hypotheses produced by biographical researchers are tied up with the kinds of sampling they use and how they frame their cases. The way a case is framed by a researcher will guide his/her case selection. For instance, contrastive comparison is worked through an iterative process in which samples are selected in relation to the wealth of the information they provide according to the criteria the researcher has posed during the research process, not before the onset of the research. One version of this process is "maximum variation sampling", in which the aim is to collect data from all perspectives and dimensions constituting the studied phenomenon. Identification of diversity is not usually obtained in a one-shot procedure before the research has been carried out; rather, the cases are selected in an iterative way while the research is in progress. Antecedent analyzed cases inform the researcher about the diversity of the following cases that have to be selected. Nevertheless, the best-known version of sampling used by RBR is Glaser and Strauss' "theoretical sampling" (1967), in which researchers select cases by relying either on minimizing differences among cases in order to describe in depth and detail a process ("mechanism") and its scope conditions, or on maximizing differences among cases in order to bring to light various versions of the studied phenomenon by identifying relevant mechanisms.

In addition, if the researcher wants a fuller picture of the studied phenomenon, he/she must implement "extreme case sampling", which is usually used for exploratory reasons, that is, as a way of explaining how an outcome has been produced, or of highlighting the effects of an event or situation. Similarly, when a case presents unexpected or surprising properties in relation either to a theory or to common sense, it is called "deviant case sampling". Gerring (2007) believes that the best way to choose a deviant case is to pose the following question: With regard to what factors is case A deviant? What is important is that both the extreme and the deviant case have an exploratory function to perform. Deviant cases' merit is that they bring to light novel aspects of a phenomenon and that they enrich researchers' theoretical ideas for explaining evidence not explained by currently known theories. We believe that social researchers should capitalize on deviant cases because generative mechanisms come to the fore more visibly in periods of crisis or transition.

Most case-oriented researchers have commented on the value of what they term crucial cases. According to Eckstein (1975, 118), a crucial case is one "that must closely fit a theory if one is to have confidence in the theory's validity, or, conversely, must not fit equally well any rule contrary to that proposed". Crucial cases can be either "most likely" or "least likely". Gerring (2007) argues that a "most likely" case is one that, on all dimensions except the dimension of theoretical interest, is predicted to achieve a certain outcome, yet it does not. It is therefore used to disconfirm a theory. By contrast, a "least likely" case is one that, on all dimensions except the dimension of theoretical interest, is predicted not to achieve a certain outcome, yet it does. It is therefore used to confirm a theory. The contribution of "most likely" and "least likely" cases is that researchers are able to broaden or narrow the scope conditions of a causal proposition or to propose new types and sub-types through the inclusion of additional variables and thereby refine a contingent generalization.

We believe that the main idea springing from what we have set out thus far is that the kind of generalizability of the causal relations discovered depends on the sampling reasoning sustaining the research design. For instance, in typical case sampling, the generalizing reasoning is of the logic "since this causal relation applies to this case, it probably applies to similar cases". This logic has been described by Lincoln and Guba (1985) as "transferability". In maximum variation and theoretical sampling, the generalizing reasoning is that typologies identify necessary and sufficient conditions through which causal relations take a different form analogously to the type. In extreme or deviant case sampling, the generalizing reasoning concerns causal relations explaining new phenomena through theory development.

Given that most of these procedures are comparative, we hold that they may culminate either A) in typological theorizing or B) in the theoretical generalizing of a process or causal chain. We illustrate below through specific examples how this can be done in the context of biographical research.

An example of typological theorizing

The example comes from Monika Wohlrab-Sahr's "Converting to Islam in Germany and USA" (1999), in which the conversion processes that take place in these two countries are investigated. Transcribed biographical interviews with men and women converts (19 from Germany and 23 from the United States) and field notes taken by the researcher from attending Muslim rituals and places of worship constitute her main research material. Some of the research questions are the following: What is the function of religious conversion within the context of converts' biographies? To what biographically rooted problems does conversion constitute a solution? What are the elements of Islam that are appropriate for dealing with typical bio-graphical problems? Why do people socialized in Western values search for solutions connected with non-Western religions? By reconstructing various biographical cases, Wohlrab-Sahr's aim is to trace the typical structures of becoming a convert in cases where it is regarded as the best solution to problems triggered by biographical developments. A biographical function is not identified through the personal motives and explanations provided by the converts themselves, but rather traced through the biographical cases' latent meaning structure (LMS). In addition, the word "function" is not used to denote a causal relation between conversion and decision making but how what is at stake concerns how the decision to convert is the outcome of previously sequential biographical decisions and their consequences. The uncovering of LMS is supported by Luhman's term "functional equiva-lents", defined as the various possibilities available as equivalent solutions for dealing with the same problem.

Wohlrab-Sahr starts by analyzing the biographical material with the aim of uncovering the LMS shaping this specific case. Reconstructing the case's structure provides an explanatory framework for understanding the bio-graphical function of converting or, in other words, for understanding the function conversion plays as a problem-solving mechanism in the face of peculiar biographical situations. After analyzing each biography, she con-structs a typology by using the operations of contextualizing and of abstrac-tion. On the one hand, the range of abstraction is gradually increasing so that each type covers as many biographies as possible and on the other, the researcher narrows her thematic focus to the biographical function of conversion. The transition from the level of case structure to the level of constructing types is enabled through the use of theoretical concepts that provide the researcher with the thematic frameworks for expanding the range of abstraction, as they constitute the axes for reconstructing indi-vidual cases, for type delimitation and for comparing types. Wohlrab-Sahr constructs types through the following four axes:

- "The reference problem", concerning the problem for which conversion functions as a solution;
- "The structure of problem solving", concerning the peculiar characteristics of problem solving;
- "The importance of the environment", concerning the role of the environment ("significant others") in shaping conversion;
- "The context of the religion", concerning the aspects of Islam described that by means of conversion are highlighted as a way to solve biographically embedded problems.

Wohlrab-Sahr mentions three main types emerging from the biographical material and corresponding to three typical forms that conversion to Islam takes whenever it functions as a response to biographically rooted problems. Converts of the first type (type A) have to deal with problems of biographical disruption related to acts of sexual offence. In such cases, conversion to Islam compensates for stigma and social devaluation within a community with extremely strict moral codes. Converts of the second type (type B) have to face frustration problems related to their failure to be upwardly mobile through education. Such frustration is experienced as a personal failure because individuals live "in limbo" in the sense that they are neither the persons they aspire to become nor the persons they were in their family of origin. Finally, converts of the third type (type C) have to overcome estrangement originating in the gap between imagining living in an ideal community and living within an individualistic society. The following Figure 5.1 depicts these three types of conversion and the problems solved by each of them:

Through this typology, Wohlrab-Sahr summarizes her findings by focusing on the various forms the logic of conversion to Islam may take. This logic becomes clear within the context of the specifics of each biography and in the face of the other "functional equivalents" that the agents did

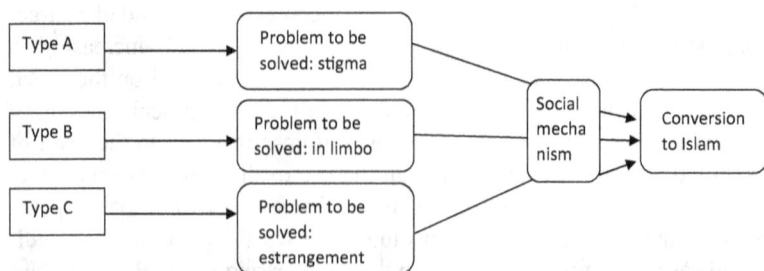

Figure 5.1 Wohlrab-Sahr'S typological theorizing on religious conversion.

not choose. The merit of typological theorizing in this example lies in its specification of the configurations of causes that lead from one situation to another. As George and Bennett (2005, 236) have argued, typological theories specify the pathways though which particular types relate to specified outcomes regardless of whether "the path has occurred only once, a thousand times or is merely hypothesized as a potential path that has not yet occurred". In addition, typological theorizing entails claims about causal mechanisms. In the above example, Wohlrab-Sahr highlights the relational mechanism that has to do with the fact that Islam provides agents with symbolic capital for recontextualizing painful, disorienting or disruptive experiences and for biographical re-orientation. Becoming a member of a new religion offers the means of a radical symbolic transformation through which agents become familiar with the "Other" and are able to deal with the problems of estrangement and discriminations they face within their own contexts.

Two examples of generalizing processes

The first example is drawn from the literature on conversion processes in order to clarify the combination of causal conditions that lead to a specific outcome. The research has been undertaken by Lofland and Rodney (1965), who state that there is a specific necessary but not sufficient condition for religious conversion to take place: a gap between ambition and reality has to be experienced by the agent, a sense of deprivation or frustration connected with how the agent would like his/her life to be and with what he/she really lives. However, this tension does not always lead to conversion because there are alternative ways of coping with it, like political recruitment or getting involved in psychotherapeutic discourses. Where neither of these options is available, then the agent is inclined to become a religious seeker and, should this situation last a long time, then he/she will start thinking either that past ways of life have been completed, that they have failed or have been disorganized, or that they are satisfactory. During this bifurcation period, agents are likely to develop emotional bonds with the new cult and to adopt their new worldview. Lofland and Rodney's example shows how BR can be used to craft a path-dependent analysis so that a theoretical proposition can be formulated regarding how people deal with turning points that may function as a causal hypothesis for future testing or refinement. The causal chain sustaining this path can be depicted as in Figure 5.2:

The second example is taken from the German sociologist Fritz Schütze (1999) and colleagues, who have forged a processual model of "suffering". By "trajectory of suffering", the authors mean the process of experiencing painful, life-disrupting situations. By investigating their subjects' varied

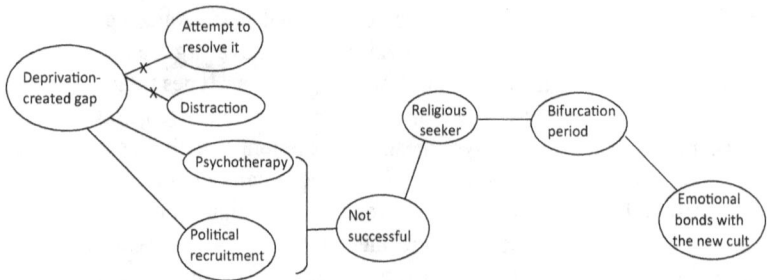

Figure 5.2 The causal process of becoming a converter.

disruptive experiences, such as mental illness, disability, drug addiction, migration and educational difficulties, the authors develop a theoretical model describing the typical stages and the developmental mechanisms of these "trajectories" (substantive theoretical models). At a more abstracted level, however, these substantive models can culminate – via contrastive comparing social processes of various substantive theoretical models – to become a formal theory capable of comprehending the phenomenon of "suffering trajectory" as a whole. The structural properties of these suffering biographical processes are the following (Schütze 1999; Riemann and Schütze, 1991):

- Built-up of trajectory potential: Specific conditions are created gradually in which the dynamics of a "trajectory" are accumulated. These conditions undermine the "taken for granted-ness" and the normal development of life by triggering disrupting tendencies which, in this first stage, remain invisible, although they signal what follows.
- Crossing the border from an intentional to a conditional state of mind: The dynamics of a "trajectory", which in the previous stage operated at a latent level, come to the fore and are expressed in various events that agents are unable to handle or control. As a result, subjects lose their agency to actively organize their everyday life and are overwhelmed by a sense of confusion and disorientation.
- Precarious new balance of everyday life: Having experienced these shocks, subjects try to restore the balance in their vulnerable everyday life. This new balance remains unstable because the crucial factors of the "trajectory" are difficult to manage.
- Breakdown of self-orientation: This unstable balance is unsettling because unexpected events are presented which agents cannot tame. Subjects try in vain to restore the balance by expending all their energy,

but the end result is chaos because of the unpredictable character of these events. The ordering of everyday life has collapsed and lots of problems make the subjects distrustful of their own expectations. They doubt their familiarity with their lifeworld and their faith in significant others is lost.

- Attempts of theoretically coming to terms with the trajectory: Subjects realize that the usual biographical resources for managing one's life do not work anymore. There is need for a radically new definition of the life situation.
- Practical working upon or escaping from the trajectory: Subjects try to put the "suffering trajectory" under control or become liberated from it by limiting its negative effects.

These stages are the essential elements of a theoretical model depicting the typical evolution of biographical stages that bear the mark of a "trajectory". The merit of such a model is that it enables researchers to trace the biographical processes occurring in various cases of the phenomenon of interest, the common features of which are suffering and a loss of familiarity with everyday life. In addition, the usage of such a model is heuristic for analyzing new aspects of the phenomenon and is open to reformulations as fresh evidence becomes available.

From what we have said thus far, we can highlight six determinants of what it means to think causally in qualitative research:

- Identify the sequence of events making up the developmental path of an outcome, by providing a detailed causal narrative of the processes involved or an explicit explanatory hypothesis;
- Discover the different causal paths that lead to similar outcomes and explore the conditions under which similarity or variance in the initial condition leads to different outcomes;
- By using comparative logic (compare cases sharing a given outcome and then identify their shared causal conditions and/or compare cases sharing a specific causal condition and then examine whether these (sufficient) cases exhibit the same outcome), one can identify causal connections between causal (necessary and sufficient) conditions and outcomes;
- Identify how mechanism and context interact in various cases or within a case;
- Bring to light how causal conditions interact through the use of typological theorizing;
- Use deviant cases to refine already existing variables or to discover new dimensions in a concept.

In order to see how these principles can be implemented as part of biographical methods, let us clarify some points. First, keep in mind that within a critical realist framework, how one experiences the world is one thing and the events of which he/she is a part or in which he/she participates constitute quite another. This means that by researching biographical material, the researcher tries to highlight the context-specific entities of which the properties define the relations within which the agent's life is deployed. Second, the necessary and sufficient conditions within which entities' powers are actualized may be identified through biographical research by tracing the generative mechanisms that implement them. Generative mechanisms show how these powers give shape to experienced life history because, as we analyzed in the previous chapters, in the social world powers depend on mechanisms that relate one (or more) entity to another (or more). In this way, by observing the lived experiences occurring within biographical trajectories, one can grasp the processes taking place at the deeper level of the "actual". This line of reasoning is based on the critical realist idea that (potential) mechanisms are latent and not manifest or observable and still have a causal effect. It is the peculiarity of the forms that triggers the potentiality of mechanisms to be actualized in specific contexts. By means of this methodological emphasis, one has a firm ground for tracing the transformative or reproductive dynamic of specific biographical forms.

Third, in contrast both to positivists who compare percentage variations in the independent and in the dependent variables and to constructivists who provide thick descriptions, a critical realist conception of RBR sets in motion abduction and retroduction. Retroduction is an inferential move from the empirical domain to the generative mechanisms played out at the actual or real level and its core element is related to abstraction, which one should not confuse with data enforcement. It seeks to ascertain what the world must be like in order for the mechanisms we observe to be as they are and not otherwise. This often involves first identifying patterns over periods of time and in different contexts to creatively ask "What if?" in order to identify often hidden causal mechanisms. Abduction refers to the redescription of how the differing elements of a phenomenon are combined in such a way as to affect events. As Danermark et al. (2002) note, abduction involves combining observations, often although not inevitably in tandem with theory, to produce the most plausible explanation of the mechanisms that caused the events. Redescription means that researchers observe, describe, interpret and explain something within the frame of a new context. It does not mean that one discovers something that nobody knew anything about before, but rather that what is discovered is "connections and relations, not directly observable, by which one can understand and explain already known occurrences in a novel way" (Danermark et al. 2002, 91).

Making comparisons, analyzing deviant cases and choosing the appropriate type of qualitative ("purposive") sampling represent the best ways to identify how a mechanism operates within a context or within the contexts compared. O'Mahoney and Vincent (2014) note that researchers may specify the relation between mechanism and context and identify their dialectical interplay.[2] Comparative research strategies offer us details regarding both the nature of the mechanism and the scope condition of the variation and inform us of the extent to which outcomes are attributable to a mechanism, its context or their interaction. In contrast to both induction and deduction, which are not informative about how the social world works, abduction and retroduction, by means of the iterative interrelation between theoretical elaboration and data collection, can lead to theory development or theory refinement. Of crucial importance in order for these goals to be achieved is the acute delineation of the phenomenon of which the case studied is an instance.

Notes

1 According to Mayntz (2002), the difference between "process" and "mechanism" is that the former emphasizes the temporal nature and the dynamic character of interaction while the latter underlines "how" that interaction takes place and the stages of a process through which specific outcomes occur.
2 Iosifides (2018) has thoroughly examined the interplay of generative mechanisms and context in migration studies.

References

Apitsch, U., and L. Inowlocki. "Biographical Analysis: A German School?." In *The Turn to Biographical Methods in Social Science: Comparative Issues and Examples*, edited by P. Chamberlayne, J. Bornat, and T. Wengraf, 53–71. London and New York: Routledge, 2000.

Burawoy, M. "The Extended Case Method." *Sociological Theory* 16, no. 1 (1998): 4–33.

Burawoy, M., A. Burton, A.A. Ferguson, K.J. Fox. *Ethnography Unbound*. Berkeley: University of California Press, 1991.

Cronbach, L.J. "Beyond the Two Disciplines of Scientific Psychology." *American Psychologist* 30, no. 2 (1975): 116–27. doi:10.1037/h0076829.

Danermark, B., M. Ekstrom, L. Jakobsen, and, J. Karlsson. *Explaining Society: An Introduction to Critical Realism in the Social Sciences*. London and New York: Routledge, 2002.

Eckstein, H. "Case Studies and Theory in Political Science." In *Handbook of Political Science*, edited by F.I. Greenstein, and N.W. Polsby. Political Science: Scope and Theory, vol. 7, 94–137. Reading, Massachusetts: Addison-Wesley, 1975.

George, L.A., and A. Bennett. *Case Studies and Theory Development in the Social Sciences*. Massachusetts: MIT Press, 2005.

Gerring, J. *Case Study Research Principles and Practices*. Cambridge: Cambridge University Press, 2007.

Glaser, B.G., and A.L. Strauss. *The Discovery of Grounded Theory: Strategies for Qualitative Research*. Chicago: Aldine, 1967.

Iosifides, T. "Epistemological Issues in Qualitative Migration Research: Self-Reflexivity, Objectivity and Subjectivity." In *Qualitative Research in European Migration Studies*, edited by R. Zapata-Barrero, and E. Yalaz, 93–113. New York: Springer, 2018.

Lincoln, Y.S., and E. Guba. *Naturalistic Inquiry*. London: Sage Publications, 1985.

Lofland, J., and S. Rodney. "Becoming a World-Saver: A Theory of Conversion to a Deviant Perspective." *American Sociological Review* 30, no. 6 (1965): 862–75.

Mayntz, R. "Zur Theoriefähigkeit makro-sozialer Analysen." In *Akteure – Mechanismen – Modelle. Zur Theoriefähigkeit makro-sozialer Analysen*, edited by R. Mayntz, 7–43. Frankfurt/M: Suhrkamp, 2002.

Mitchell, J.C. "Case and Situation Analysis." *Sociological Review* 31, no. 2 (1983): 187–211. doi:10.3102/0013189X033002003.

O'Mahoney, J., and S. Vincent. "Critical Realism as an Empirical Project: A Beginner's Guide." In *Putting Critical Realism Into Practice: A Guide to Research Methods in Organizational Studies*, edited by P. Edwards, J. O'Mahoney, and S. Vincent, 1–21. London: Oxford University Press, 2014.

Przyborsky, A., and M. Wohlrab-Sahr. *Qualitative Sozialforschung*. 3rd ed. München: Oldenburg, 2010.

Riemann, G., and F. Schütze. "'Trajectory' as a Basic Theoretical Concept for Analyzing Suffering and Disorderly Social Processes." In *Social Organization and Social Process : Essays in Honor of Anselm Strauss*, edited by D.R. Maines, 333–57. New York: de Gruyter, 1991. https://nbn-resolving.org/urn:nbn:de:016 8-ssoar-7214.

Rosenthal, G. *Interpretive Social Research*. Göttingen: Göttingen University Press, 2018.

Schütze, F. "Verlaufskurven des Erleidens als Forschungsgegenstand der interpretativen Soziologie." In *Handbuch erziehungswissenschaftliche Biographieforschung*, edited by H.-H. Krüger, and W. Marotzki, 191–223. Opladen: Leske + Budrich, 1999.

Siouti, I. "Biography as a Theoretical and Methodological Key Concept in Transnational Migration Studies." In *The Routledge International Handbook on Narrative and Life History*, edited by I. Godson, A. Antikainen, M. Andrews, and P. Sikes, 179–90. Abingdon: Routledge, 2017.

Small, L.M. "'How many cases do I need?' on Science and the Logic of Case Selection in Field-Based Research." *Ethnography* 10, no. 1 (2009): 5–38. doi:10.1177/1466138108099586.

Wohlrab-Sahr, M. *Konversion zum Islam in Deutschland und USA*. Frankfurt/M.: Campus, 1999.

6 The relational subject and latent meaning structures

Up to this point our line of reasoning has underlined the relevance of three interrelated ideas: first, we developed a mechanism-based approach to causality which is at odds with methodological individualism; second, in order to enrich this idea we showed how the relational nature of the social, the causal power of its emergent properties and the identification of synchronic and diachronic relations make specific things happen; and third, we brought to light the role that temporality plays in creating necessary and sufficient conditions within which relations take specific forms and not others. In the next two chapters we develop how these ideas constitute the socio-ontological and epistemological ground for claiming causal explanations through biographical research. To this end, we must identify specific theoretical axes on which causality-inspired and interpretivism-driven biographical research intersect.

From the repertoire of the various theoretical traditions through which biographical research is implemented, we focus here on reconstructive biographical research (RBR), the distinguishing feature of which is not only the description of agents' perspectives, but mostly their explanation: by studying biographies and life stories one can identify latent meaning structures (LMS), which explain either agents' life orientations and life projects or the ways in which they experience social events. LMS perform two functions: on the one hand, they structure action dispositions and plans of an agent and on the other, they sustain the coherence and the continuity of his/her biographical identity. In addition, they can be presented both as *opus operatum* – as they are the crystallization of a lifelong process of practical, embodied engagement with the world's objects, of social acting as well as of involvement in social relations – and as *opus operandi*, to the extent that they function as a generative structure forming agents' experiences and actions (see also Silkenbeumer and Wernet 2010).

The main thesis we defend is that "latent meaning structures" constitute the *par excellence* intersection point at which a mechanism-based approach to causality and the interpretivist epistemology meet and upon which one can build causal explanations through RBR. The term has its origins in Oevermann's Objective Hermeneutic (OH).[1] Oevermann tried to synthesize two seemingly different conceptions of social reality: those that prioritize the meaningfulness of the social and those that refuse to identify meanings with how agents attribute meanings to their actions and tend to exhaust their analysis in how consciousness constructs objects. For interpretivists the goal of social research is to disclose the subjectively attributed meaning of social action. By contrast, OH aims at uncovering how LMS are the generative matrices of actions.

It is here that one can identify two points of similarity between OH and critical realism's (CR) social ontology: in relation to the idea that a lived experience is *a priori* inter-subjective and relational and not individual, because first, agents attribute meaning not to the singular Other but to the meaning their relationship has and, second, relationships take forms whose properties affect the action of their parts causally. He puts forward the idea that the distinctive property of social relations is their latency in the sense that latency transcends the human beings composing them and has to be conceived as a potentiality of humans, not as a psychoanalytic unconscious. By conceptualizing the social in this way, one avoids the criticism of essentialism because relations are "accidents" and not "essences". Instead of dividing the world into entities like the "social" and the "individual" and then trying to connect them, relational social ontology takes into account both people's singularity and relations' causal efficacy (Donati 2011).

Furthermore, RBR and critical realism share the idea that meaning structures are ontologically independent of the individual in the sense that meanings become independent through time and are crystallized in the institutional forms within which individuals live. For Oevermann the term "objective" concerns not the method but the object of hermeneutic reconstruction, which is nothing other than the meaning structures that exist independently of agents' interpretations and of their intentions (Bohnsack 1999). However, independence should not be seen as the outcome of disembodied discourses but as the emergent effect produced by humans while they are interacting. Our position is that humans' reasons for actions are real and causal, but not capable of explaining higher-level phenomena. This means that it is one thing to acknowledge agents' temporal priority, relational autonomy and causal efficacy and quite another to identify the generative mechanisms that explain their shaping. The point that needs to be stressed is the non-reductive character of these two levels: social reality cannot be reduced to agents' transactions and this explains why CR's relational approach should not be confused with relativism. As Porpora (2018, 425) puts it, "power, and privilege are not behaviors but relational conditions underlying behavior" meaning that social arrangements (pre)exist which prescribe peculiar situations for acting out power and privilege".

In a similar vein, OH favours the critical realist distinction between the transitive and the intransitive level of analysis, because meaning structures, although emergent, are crystallized as such only at the intransitive level of the real, not at the level of the empirical and on agents' consciousness. In other words, meaning structures for OH emerge over time, via the social forms through which individuals pass during the course of their life. This means that both OH and CR prioritize the relational nature of lived experience through which meaning structures emerge. In our view, what is at stake is not how the old-fashioned dualism agency/structure can be overcome but how a viable conceptualization of the relational nature of the social can be viable for social research and, especially to our project, for RBR. We elaborate this point by focusing on how RBR and a relational sociology make sense of socialization.

For OH, subjects are socialized by means of selectively and gradually reconstructing the (explicit and tacit) rules of their social interaction within which they position themselves and through which they shape their motivational universe. Despite the fact that agents are depicted as capable of decoding meaning by relying on their own powers, we suggest that there exists a surplus of meaning within this nexus of rules that transcends this power. This is why the wealth of meaning that emerges in social relations is something quite different from how agents make sense of them or try to alter them. We believe that it is not culture's omnipotence of being interiorized through its rules (as a discursive constructionist would claim) that causes agents' actions, but their power to select specific socializing contents that are existentially connected with their biographical details. Reflexivity is what enables agents to select the social influences that "fit" with their social profile and to project future actions. This idea is propounded by Archer (2004), who disputes constructivists' contention that humans are motivated through the voices provided by various discourses, because in this way they subscribe to a contractual conception of socialization that is incapable of explaining social or identity change. By refusing to approach the social genesis of the subject both as a rational actor to whom society offers only "situations" and as a discursive voice, Archer thinks that what these approaches miss is the experience of reality *per se* and that this reality is replaced with how it is perceived, either in instrumental or in contractual terms.

Critical realists call this replacement "epistemic fallacy", whereby what really exists and how one has access to it are conflated. By contrast, for critical realists, that which exists (ontologically) has a regulatory effect upon what we make of it and, in turn, what it makes of us. A similar idea has been advanced by Oevermann et al. (1979, 367) when they refer to "two levels of reality: the reality of a text's LMS which can be reconstructed independently of each mental representation of the producer or the recipient of the text and the reality of agents' subjective meanings which are intentionally presented in a text". In order to clarify how the reality of LMS is mediated by the contingent reality of social relations, Oevermann draws upon structuralism's theory of text analysis, specifically the structural level, which corresponds to the "grammar" of social reality, while contingent actions are populated by how subjects make sense of it.[2] This idea is similar to Donati and Archer's (2015) claim that the externality of expectations is a precondition for the emergence of consciousness. This is not to be confused with Wittgenstein's "language games" because first, Archer (2015a) sees individuals as equipped with liabilities existing as possibilities, the development of which depends upon the form of social relations and, second, she emphasizes that one's sense of self stems from one's practical engagement with the world's objects, which is wordless and not conceptually thematized. It is an embodied engagement through which various lines of actions are opened. Praxis, in other words, is the non-thematized source of the emergence of reasoning through which humans become familiar with the fact that the social world is populated by forces that work independently of how and whether we perceive them. It is through this process that the world of intransitive objects is formed as early as our infancy. In Dilthey's terms, objects resist how we experience them. Only on condition of the independent existence of intransitive objects is the principle of non-contradiction meaningful. The relational subject to which Archer refers emerges from wordless object relations rather than being discursively created, because such things as bodily self-consciousness and the ability to intend to objects are shared with other non-human living organisms.

As a consequence, causal influence moves not only from society to individuals but from individuals to society. Nevertheless, this is not to be seen as a voluntaristic premise but as owing to the fact that the self is an emergent and layered reality. Archer (2015b) distinguishes four levels of self-formation: the "I", the "me", the "we" and the "you". The "I" refers to the continuity of the sensing self over time. It is not about biological or social continuity but rather the sense that it is I who can construe myself independently of others' interpretations. For Archer, this is an ontological position, not an epistemological one as always favoured by constructivists. This means that the self gets the sense that he/she is a body that goes through various situations during its life course and that he/she does not have access to all the causes that shaped him/her. In this way, the "I" can not be considered only as "narratively constructed" as radical constructivists believe, because thereby reflexivity and how the "I" copes with the world are not taken into consideration. On the other hand, the "me" concerns how the self sees him/herself from the standpoint of others. In this way, the "I" identifies the sense of continuity and change over time while the "me" has an objective dimension as it refers to external perceptions. The "you" refers to how the "I" develops orientations towards the future or the "not yet" throughout his/her life.

We believe that the most intriguing element of Archer's analysis is the temporal nature of self-formation, because it can frame a life course perspective that takes into consideration the fact that people are born into specific class conditions connected to impediments and facilitations from which specific life chances are opened. The "I" becomes gradually familiar with the objects of the "me", some of which matter whereas others do not and are resistant to change. This means that the "I" discovers the external world in an emotionally charged way and becomes involved with others with whom he/she gets the sense of "we". The "we" concerns social groups and social relations whose emergent properties exert a causal influence on the "I" due to the peculiar features that they present and through which the "you", that is, the future self, is formed. It is within these nexuses of relationships that stocks of meanings are produced and by means of which agents project their actions.

Two of the most crucial things affecting humans when they enter the world are first, that they explore it in a embodied manner and second, by being attributed a name ("you are Lisa, the daughter of Martha" is the "me") and various roles from their environment, they achieve a sense of belonging to various collective entities as they grow up (family) and form the notion of a "we" (achieved by belonging to an "us"). Once humans personify their roles, they develop their ultimate concerns (the things that they care about most) and gradually, while passing through various social relations, develop the "you" by reflecting upon past, present and future orientations. Donati argues (2011) that ultimate concerns are the answers given to the existential questions that people ask of themselves when they consider their own happiness and their desire for a "good life" for themselves. In this way, people's goals are imbued with these concerns when they take critical decisions for their lives. For the practice of RBR, this means that in making sense of agents' decision-making processes, researchers have to take into account the totality of the dimensions of self throughout their lives. To the extent that ultimate concerns are the key to understanding these processes, they have to be explored in conjunction with agents "me", "we" and "you". Ultimate concerns are relationally conceived and not as a solipsistic "I" facing the world.

However, the meanings that emerge in these nexuses are always surplus in the sense that they have an additional element of which people make sense. Given that in their everyday lives agents act in a pre-reflective and restricted manner due to specific time and space resources, they are unable to grasp the totality of these meanings, which become latent over time. In other words, the meanings produced in social relationships are one thing and the intentional meanings crafted by the agents are quite another. In the same way that in Archer's theory meanings emerge within specific forms of social relations beyond individuals' construal, OH's distinction of objective meaning from individuals' intentions constitutes its emblematic idea. We have to note that what separates the radical social constructivist identification of intentions with the language of Archer's and OH's positions is that this surplus of meaning is rooted not in language but in social practice and in the form of social relationships. Hence, to the extent that the self is composed of emergent and relational properties that are realized through his/her embodied and wordless engagement with the social world's objects, it follows that there is a surplus of meaning that surpasses agents' intentions and that leaves its mark upon them. In other words, LMS in OH represent the non-propositional knowledge of practical involvement in the world through which the "you" is formed and which leaves its traces. The reason for this surpassing is connected to the historicity of experience and to the emergent features of the forms of social relations in which agents live during the course of their lives.

One should not view LMS through the Lacanian unconscious which is "structured as language", but as practical knowledge obtained in an embodied manner that resembles a stock found "in the seat of our pants rather than in the declarative memory, and that … may be accessed by all of our senses, not just by one part – the auditory system" (Archer 2004, 160). In this way, consciousness refers not to itself but to something "out there", because language concerns not only its usage but its practical acquisition as well. Saying that language is a self-referential system enclosed from the external world means that one remains oblivious to the above-mentioned concept of "ultimate concerns" and to distinguishing right from wrong, true from false and valuable from invaluable. However, people in the real world live their lives through these distinctions. Within this life course grounding of ultimate concerns, a crucial distinction has to be underlined: that personal identity is different from but dialectically related to social identity, meaning that people's ultimate concerns about what matters to them interact with their social concerns. As Archer has stated (2006, as cited in Donati 2011, 52), our personal identities are not reducible to mere gifts of society. In the process, our social identity also becomes defined, but necessarily as a subset of personal identity.

This idea is underscored by OH through what is termed "case structure", a core concept of its research programme. Every specific case is peculiar to the extent that it has been shaped through specific selectivity processes enabled by the possibilities connected to particular social fields. As Wohlrab-Sahr (1999) puts it, a case structure is formed to the extent that specific possibilities are selected while others are excluded even though they could have been selected, too. In addition, a case structure is created over time because a specific type of selection is repeated and, in this way, specific anticipations are established.[3] Thus, it is inferred that the range of possible options concerning an action is framed by the nexus of rules tied up with a specific field. In other words, LMS constitute the internal logic of every specific case, upon which its essential pattern rests. This means that none of its manifestations are a coincidence but rather have a logic peculiar to its selection processes. In this sense, the meaning structure is latent, because it has a semi-conscious and semi-habitual character. For instance, the members of a family follow specific rituals, talk about habitual issues and are part of specific struggles within their kinship. These are all features that constitute a family's way of being in the world, providing them with a sense of routine and predictability. However, the members of the family do not use these practices and rituals in order to attain a sense of stability, predictability and routine; rather, these seem to be the unintended consequences of their actions, the principle of which is not to be found in the agents' unconscious. They come to the fore only in cases of crisis or of intense self-reflection and resemble what is termed "tacit knowledge". Stated bluntly, a surplus of meaning is not found in language but in social practice and in practical involvement with particular things. As Archer (2004, 156) notes, when one says to his/her beloved, "You look like a rose", he/she is not denoting the truth value of propositional knowledge, but an embodied knowledge and a practical relation with a thing by means of which his/her senses have been trained to communicate his/her love through a metaphor.

CR and OH converge not only in the idea that the world is the site where the stock of knowledge and LMS are formed but also in how they make sense of the *par excellence* concept upon which biographical research is structured: lived experience. Instead of identifying lived experience with the perception of experience and with internal processes, CR and OH conceive of it as a relational being-with-others experience. "Lived experience" in this sense is temporally and relationally constituted once it is characterized as an effort of the human being to adapt to the environment by changing it. This adaptation has to be seen as a projection because humans think forwards into the unknown to make it known. Hence, experience opens up new possibilities by seeking new directions through the use of the wholeness of human beings like sensation, emotion, cognition, volition and conation. Archer's "relational subject" (2015b) is in line with this conception of lived experience as she makes sense of "being in relation" as referring to three things.

First, that between the "I" and the "alter" is a distance that differentiates and binds them at the same time; second, that their relation is real and
reducible neither to the "I" nor to the "alter"; and third, that their relation
takes a form connected with specific emerging properties that have specific
causal powers. This is what Archer means when she says that these emerging properties entail both reproduction (morphostasis) and transformation
(morphogenesis) for the reason that agents are open to reflecting upon the
alter's influences and upon the relation itself in order to change it. However,
it would be wrong to reduce social relations to how people use symbols
to make projections, because they are something broader and different.
According to a critical realist stance, they are invisible but real entities, not
as a Durkheimian would understand them but as a Simmelian would frame
them, namely as an effect of mutuality or reciprocity (Papilloud 2018).
Given that humans have the power to form relations, researchers have to
take it into consideration in order to ascertain what takes place within. Once
the unit of analysis becomes a social relation, one obtains a deeper insight
into "whether, where, and how society exceeds itself beyond the recurring crises it goes through, creating new historical-societal configurations"
(Donati 2015, 3). For instance, it is not unusual for agents faced with critical
biographical moments or turning points to thematize their tacit knowledge
and to take decisions that transform their relations. Social change is the
outcome of these transformations and of the transformations upon the generative mechanisms that shape social relations. Relations have the power to
affect the motives of the "I" and the "alter" and to trigger minor or major
changes. Relations have the property of openness, the outcomes of which
are not easily predicted, whether via behavioural stimuli or psychological
beliefs. This explains the unintended consequences of actions, the generative mechanisms of which are to be found not in belief formation but in the
emerging properties of social relations. This is why the outcome of a relationship may be completely at odds with individuals' motives on the basis
of which the relation started. Buckley (1954, 42) was the first to clarify this
idea with the following words:

> When we say that 'the whole is more than the sum of its parts,' the
> meaning becomes unambiguous and loses its mystery: the 'more than'
> points to the fact of organization, which imparts to the aggregate char-
> acteristics that are not only different from, but often not found in the
> components alone; and the 'sum of the parts' must be taken to mean,
> not their numerical addition, but their unorganized aggregation.

Insofar as the emphasis shifts from "lived experience" to the "relational subject", it follows that RBR's programme is empowered against the criticisms

raised by radical constructivists. Instead of reconstructing a subjective point of view, emphasis is paid to identifying the mechanisms that form biographical trajectories. Moreover, instead of researching subjective meaning, what is researched concerns how the various social relations that are formed over time and from which relational properties emerge affect groups' trajectories and people's biographical decision making. Biographical research understood through the framework of relational sociology does not reduce "lived experience" to a mere storytelling activity or communication, but rather conceives of it as a "trace" left by past and present forms of social relations. By analyzing this trace, researchers can access the surplus of meaning that constitutes the emergent effect of these forms. The objectivity of meaning is rooted in these emerging relational properties and not in the individual's sense-making process. Meaning objectivity is not to be seen as a situational achievement based on individual needs, but rather things take the opposite direction: agents' intentions take shape within an intersubjectively shared web of meanings and rules that permeate specific face-to-face interactions. Meaning objectivity, in other words, is not the aggregative summation of agents' beliefs, but rather is made out of the nexus of relations whose parts are connected through specific configurations and from which specific patterns of possible meanings stem. As a result, every new action is not just added to previous ones, but rather informs future actions in specific ways to the extent of opening up new possibilities for action while foreclosing others. The regulative process of this openness is framed by the LMS that organize agents' decision making. In this sense, RBR's aim is to reconstruct the peculiar selectivity processes that characterize a case and to trace the peculiar logic that sustains agents' choices, which over time are patterned. The singularity of a case can be understood only if the researcher takes into consideration those lines of action that even though they could have been chosen, were not.

This way of approaching biographical meaning is similar to how Simmel (1950) makes sense of the relation between social forms and psychological contents. By researching people's biographical details, one is not studying just psychological contents but is trying to capture the conditions of possibility that enable specific forms of association to take place. By studying forms of social relations, biographical research as enacted through the lens of RBR investigates the "in between" of humans' lives by specifying how the LMS of each biographical case takes shape through various forms of relations in agents' life history. In chapter 8 we provide methodological elaborations as to how this goal can be achieved, but for now it suffices to say that LMS represent the link connecting biographical cases with the formal properties of the relational mechanisms as they emerge in people's relations. As Cantó-Milà (2018) has argued, this "in between" element of sociality has been conceptualized by Simmel through three apriorities. First, people apprehend each other through typifying schemes, enabling them to experience the "you" as real and immediate, or as taken for granted. This typifying capacity is what enables people to build wholes of the "you" made out of fragments. However, second, there is always a non-social element that is not socially communicable and ungraspable from this building capacity. Third, human beings experience the social relations in which they live both by looking forwards and looking backwards. This is the most promising idea for RBR and Simmel thinks that one way to understand this is through how one chooses a vocation/profession for the reason that one can see his/her profession either as something he/she has to do due to family tradition or as something by which to realize future life projects. In both cases, the interplay of looking forwards and looking backwards is the cohering ground for experiencing the present. The explanation of social phenomena entails the capturing of social forms by researching specific social relations. The psychological contents are interesting for researchers because they afford access to the forms of relations of which people are members. The Kantian influences are obvious here because social forms are captured by the researcher by way of abstraction. RBR, by approaching biographies as thematic and temporal wholes, tries to reconstruct the formal features of the phenomenon of interest. "Formal" here is neither identical to language structures nor to the linguistic genres used by storytellers, but rather to the relational and emergent properties of their real-life social relations in which they live their lives.

The reason behind such an emphasis is nothing other than the fact that Simmel identifies the explanatory matrix of the social with the detailed capturing of these relational properties of social forms. This means that social forms constitute a reality that can be studied on its own terms, or in a similar parlance; they are an irreducible reality presenting higher-order properties. In this sense, LMS represent a relational term referring to peculiar features of people's relations considered on their own. As we analyzed in the previous chapters, reductionism and conflation are the two dangers one has to avoid. Donati (2015) has highlighted the misunderstandings that emerge when one tries to captures relationality as a *per se* reality through the use of language alone. The best-known outcome of this misunderstanding is indeterminacy, namely that relations are free-floating entities created by coincidence. However, this is far from that which relational epistemology wants to dissociate. The concept of "generative mechanisms" protects one from committing this fallacy by identifying the causal path through which specific things to people's biographies take place. As we mentioned in the first chapter, one does not need to accept the covering law model in order to identify causal mechanisms for the cases that are covered by this model, let alone those that are not. Singular causal mechanisms enable one to identify the formal features of social relations by means of which agents' selectivity processes take a specific route and not another. People's biographies are made of relations that take diverse forms, such as family, school, kin and friendship networks, job roles or various other groups. People are more or less involved in a decision-making process in order to make up their minds. The explanatory route of these selectivity processes is to be found in the relational traces connected to the peculiarities of the forms of the relations in which they have lived. What the researcher analyzes, however, is not solely biographical narratives but mostly social relations' emergent mechanisms, giving birth to LMS. The meaning of a relation does not reside in the individual but in how its emergent properties affect people's selectivity processes. However, the *par excellence* cardinal question pertains to how this emergent effect comes into being. Donati thinks that the answer does not lie in what the agent's meaning refers to (*refero*) but to the bond created between the alter and the ego (*religo*). Generative mechanisms are the effect of this reciprocal relation, which is structured according to the axes of time (present/future) and space (inside/ outside). The formal properties of social relations are structured in time and space and may be seen as causal chains. Although not a scholar committed to CR, Gross (2018) has provided an account of causal chains in which different layers of contextual factors form and sustain them, but he emphasizes actions and interactions rather than relations and this is what differentiates him from CR. Nevertheless, he provides an account of how these contextual factors are structured in a layered manner: "layers near the bottom are populated by individual actors. At the intermediate levels we find medium-scale entities such as work groups, friendship networks, and local religious congregations. Large-scale collective actors are at the topmost levels: states, classes, multinational firms" (Gross 2018, 15). What he wants to stress is the sequential and temporal structure of consequences and how when triggered, processes produce outcomes. In the next chapter, we highlight the interaction of temporality with causality as conceived through the commonalities of RBR and a critical relationist perspective.

Notes

1 On OH, see Oevermann et al. (1979; 1980), Oevermann (2000), Tsiolis (2006) and Silkenbeumer and Wernet (2010).
2 For Bude (1982), this distinction resembles the paradigmatic/syntagmatic levels of analyzing narratives. LMS correspond to the paradigmatic level, where the rules are not context-specific, while subjective manifestations correspond to the syntagmatic level, as they are enacted at a specific time and in a specific place.

3 The process of structure formation and the prospects for its reproduction or transformation constitute its historical/biographical character (Wernet 2000).

References

Archer, M. *Being Human: The Problem of Agency.* Cambridge: Cambridge University Press, 2004.

Archer, M. "The Relational Subject and the Person: Self, Agent, and Actor." In *The Relational Subject*, edited by P. Donati, and M. Archer, 85–123. Cambridge: Cambridge University Press, 2015a.

Archer, M. "Socialization as Relational Reflexivity." In *The Relational Subject*, edited by P. Donati, and M. Archer, 123–55. Cambridge: Cambridge University Press, 2015b.

Bohnsack, R. *Rekonstruktive Sozialforschung. Einführung in Methodologie und Praxis qualitativer Forschung.* 3rd ed. Opladen: Leske and Budrich, 1999.

Buckley, W. *Sociology and Modern Systems Theory.* Englewood Cliffs, NJ: Prentice Hall, 1954.

Bude, H. "Text und soziale Realität." *Zeitschrift für Sozialisationsforschung & Erziehungssoziologie* 2 (1982): 134–43.

Cantó-Milà, N. "Georg Simmel's Concept of Forms of Association as an Analytical Tool for Relational Sociology." In *The Palgrave Handbook of Relational Sociology*, edited by F. Dépelteau, 217–31. New York: Palgrave Macmillan, 2018.

Donati, P. *Relational Sociology. A New Paradigm for the Social Sciences.* London and New York: Routledge, 2011.

Donati, P. "Manifesto for a Critical Realist Relational Sociology." *International Review of Sociology* 25, no. 1 (2015): 86–109. doi:10.1080/03906701.2014.9 97967.

Donati, P., and M. Archer. "Introduction: Relational Sociology: Reflexive and Realist." In *The Relational Subject*, edited by P. Donati, and M. Archer, 3–33. Cambridge: Cambridge University Press, 2015.

Gross, N. "The Structure of Causal Chains." *Sociological Theory* 36, no. 4 (2018): 1–25. doi:10.1177/0735275118811377.

Oevermann, U. "Die Methode der Fallrekonstruktion in der Grundlagenforschung sowie der klinischen und pädagogischen Praxis." In *Fallrekonstruktion: Sinnverstehen in der sozialwissenschaftlichen Forschung*, edited by K. Kraimer, 58–156. Frankfurt/M.: Suhrkamp, 2000.

Oevermann, U., T. Allert, E. Konau, and J. Krambeck. "Die Methodologie einer «Objektiven Hermeneutik» und ihre allgemeinforschungslogische Bedeutung in den Sozialwissenschaften." In *Interpretative Verfahren in den Sozial- und Textwissenschaft*, edited by H.-G. Brose, 352–434. Stuttgart: Metzler, 1979.

Oevermann, U., T. Allert, and E. Konau. "Zur Logik der Interpretation von Interviewtexten. Fallanalyse anhand eines Interviews mit einer Fernstudentin. In *Interpretationen einer Bildungsgeschichte. Überlegungen zur Sozialwissenschaftlichen Hermeneutik*, edited by T. Heinze, H.W. Klusemann, and H.-G. Soeffner, 15–69. Bensheim: Päd. Extra, 1980.

Papilloud, C. "George Simmel and Relational Sociology." In *The Palgrave Handbook of Relational Sociology*, edited by F. Dépelteau, 201–17. New York: Palgrave Macmillan, 2018.

Porpora, V.D. "Critical Realism as Relational Sociology." In *The Palgrave Handbook of Relational Sociology*, edited by F. Dépelteau, 413–31. New York: Palgrave Macmillan, 2018.

Silkenbeumer, M., and A. Wernet. "Biographische Identität und Objektive Hermeneutik: methodologische Überlegungen zum narrativen Interview." In *Subjekt – Identität – Person? Reflexionen zur Biographieforschung*, edited by B. Griese, 171–98. Wiesbaden: VS Verlag, 2010.

Simmel, G. "Fundamental Problems of Sociology. Individual and Society." In *The Sociology of Georg Simmel*, edited by W. Kurt, 3–84. New York: Free Press, 1950.

Tsiolis, G. *Life Stories and Biographical Narrations. Biographical Approach in Sociological Qualitative Research*. Athens: Kritiki (in Greek), 2006.

Wernet, A. *Einführung in die Interpretationstechnik der Objektiven Hermeneutik*. Opladen: Leske + Budrich, 2000.

Wohlrab-Sahr, M. *Konversion zum Islam in Deutschland und USA*. Frankfurt/M.: Campus, 1999.

7   Why the temporal is causal

The previous chapter demonstrated that an explanation-oriented reconstructive biographical research (RBR) can be achieved by relying on the following theoretical axes:

- Agents are beings in relation to others, relations whose forms are tied up with relational mechanisms that affect causally their parts;
- Agents' actions can be understood by taking into consideration the latent meaning structures (LMS) of which the traces are found to how social relations have been formed, which gives shape to their biographies;
- Due to 1) and 2) and because agents live their lives through various forms of relations, LMS function as a stock of knowledge that sustains their biographical construction;
- The fundamental property of agents' meaning is its latency because it has been accumulated through agents' practical involvement with the world and because agents are unaware of its functioning.

These four axes revolve around the idea that the way in which one lives his/ her life is characterized by a regularity that is not to be reduced to agents' intentions and projects and whose generality is expressed in various life situations, without it being the outcome of agents' consciousness (Bude 1998). Even in cases where peoples' choices seem incoherent, there is a unifying principle that renders them intelligible and that can be traced to the LMS. In order to deal with these seemingly inconsistent rules of biographical construction, Bude introduces a distinction between meaning and intention. In the same way that speakers mean more than what they say, agents produce by acting more meaning than they believe. Speaking and acting develop a peculiar logic that exceeds agents' initial intentions and that can be captured only *a posteriori*: In the case of the speaker, this logic emerges from agents' tacit knowledge, while in the case of actors, it takes shape due to what critical realists term "relational feedback". Both of these points can be approached through the prism of the stratified ontology of the empirical, the actual and the real. The real concerns the powers of social entities such as institutions, social groups or social relations, which may causally affect people and be affected by them. The researcher's goal is to identify the conditions under which these powers become active at the level of the actual. The actual refers to what happens if and when these powers are activated, what they do and what eventuates when they do. Finally, the empirical has to do with how agents experience their social worlds. What needs to be stressed is the distinction between observability and existence: what one perceives is one thing while what really exists is quite another. A version of critical realism (CR)-inspired biographical research can help us identify the unifying principle that gives shape to agents' biographies belonging to various social situations, groups, social classes or types of life courses. A realist ontology therefore makes it possible to understand how we can be or become many things that currently we are not: the unemployed can become employed, the ignorant can become knowledgeable and so on. Through the three-level ontology of CR one can identify the dynamics of an "unlived" life which is entailed into biographies and which, albeit at the biographer's disposal in an intuitive but not reflective way, constitutes the source of transforming the biographer's life and contexts (Alheit 2010).

From what we have said thus far it follows that it is not by accident that CR prioritizes the role of context to mechanisms' activation: the interaction between context and mechanism makes specific things happen, like decision making, life choices or new social relationships. Given that these outcomes are created through social relations' emergent powers, CR puts at the forefront a processual conception according to which mechanisms activated in specific contexts bring to life specific outcomes. This is why the ontological concept of emergence enables us to view biographies as open systems[1] prone to various possibilities and not as *a priori* determined by social forces. In addition, it enables us to go beyond a quantitative view that is limited in studying life courses because the explanatory reasoning prioritized by a CR-framed RBR looks for generative process at the level of the real, not at the observable level of statistical variables. Uncovering the hidden also constitutes the goal of RBR. Bude, for example, in answering the question of how one has access to the meaning structure unifying agents' biographies through analyzing their biographical interviews, holds that agents, besides the information they provide in an embodied way regarding various life experiences, narrate, describe, argue and express worldviews and life projects. All these biographical manifestations are interwoven and form a nexus through which the structure of their life construction discloses itself. In this sense, researchers' task is to identify and decode the internal logic of this construction. "Life construction" is the object researchers are trying to analyze through the methodological principles of structural meaning reconstruction (Bude 1987). What are the details of these principles? According to Bude, the art of interpretation lies in uncovering the unobservable and unexpected dimensions of a social phenomenon: "The correspondences among its demonstrations reveal the lawfulness of an object." (Bude 1987, 104). If the object of the interpretation is the text that stems from a social encounter in which one of the speakers reflects on his/her life history, then reconstructing a meaning structure lies in uncovering the hidden structure of this text (Bude 1998).

The main idea to which Bude's conception and CR meet concerns how they make sense of the "hidden". CR maintains that first, this "hidden" exists at the level of the real and that its causal effects are instantiated into agents' biographies, not into their intentional meanings and that second, it can be traced into the relational emergent properties of their social relations. It has been repeatedly noted that emergence has a temporal grounding in the sense that at the synchronic level, social relations' emergent properties are crystallized, while at the diachronic level, the powers of these properties leave their causal effects upon social events and shape agents' life decisions. In other words, emergent properties are sustained by causal mechanisms that act at the diachronic level. Thus, RBR is not based on a conception of "lived experience" in the traditional sense of interpretivism because this conception is limited to the level of the empirical, but it sheds light on how social events take place at the level of the actual and it prepares us for the generative mechanisms upon which LMS are formed at the level of the real. As Sawyer (2005) argues, there is more to the world than patterns of events and this "more" is the historicity of the emergence that makes latent agents' meaning structures pass as unnoticed.

Needless to say, this kind of explaining the hidden is in conflict with the explanatory reductionism conducted by those who embrace interpretivists' theory of subjective meaning or with those who take "empathy" to be the sole route to accessing meaning. As we stressed in chapter 2, explanatory reductionism explains things by reducing higher-level properties to their lower-level equivalents, while CR prioritizes how something is crystallized and how this affects people and in this sense causality for CR has a temporal dimension. This is how both critical realists and RBR conceive of the concept of structure, as both try to explore how researchers can pass from textual analysis to the tracing of LMS. To this end, Sawyer (2005) suggests posing counterfactual questions upon the material in order to analyze the interplay between context and mechanism. In particular, such questions might include:

- What are the preconditions for a specific practice/relationship/social object to become a social phenomenon (for example, what are the preconditions for the location of a playground or square to become the site of adolescent identity construction?);

- Could this specific practice/relationship/social object take shape without these preconditions (could local identity exist without the social space of a playground or square taking a social meaning or without specific forms of sociability taking place?);
- How is this specific practice/relationship/social object affected by another practice/relationship/social object (how does the motorbike culture of vocational adolescents affect the local identity of its members?)

As we previously stated, LMS represent the unifying principle underlying all the seemingly divergent life dimensions of people's life histories and have been crystallized as the biographies' internal logic through a gradual process of "selectivity". This process is what the researcher must disclose by discerning what actually took place from what could be the case so as to identify the necessary and sufficient conditions of why things took that direction and not another.

This is where RBR meets how CR approaches agents' meaning attribution to things. RBR draws upon a theoretical idea taken from systems theory connected with self-referential systems. These systems are self-referential in the sense that they perceive of external stimuli not in conformity to external influences but in accordance to their internal logic, through which they decode them. In a similar vein, Alheit and Dausien (2000) argue that "psychic systems" present a self-referential function as to how social influences are inscribed to people's biographies and are perceived. By adopting a system theory terminology, they note that "social communications" are not perceived by "psychic systems" as "inputs" producing "outputs" but as self-referential "intakes". The crucial difference is that agents experience the social by a way of "translating" it through a peculiar "code" of biographical processing. The peculiar "code" through which social reality is processed is termed "biographical construction". However, for Alheit and Dausien, biographical construction should not be identified with self-definitions or self-descriptions but as a LMS sedimented in a changing way throughout the life course.

This idea of "psychic" systems' internal logic that mediates the experiencing of the social is similar to critical realists' acknowledgment that social action is tied up with a kind of internal conversation that is relationally constituted in the sense that the self dialogues with itself in relation to the (social) context. By deliberating on the relation *per se*, agents can influence the production of social phenomena in a qualitatively different way, generating a specific range of outcomes. In order to frame this idea of relational reflexivity as a version of Taylor's "strong evaluations", Archer

(2015) holds that agents develop internal dialogues while the relations are in progress. Let us return to the terminology of the previous chapter of the "relational subject" structured in relation to the levels of "I", "you", "me" and "we", which emerge on a temporal basis. The "I" refers to the various "now"s of the self, the "me" is connected to the past images of the self and the "you" is related to the future selves. According to this temporal conception of self, people experience the present in conjunction with the "not yet" and with the "no longer", or else, in conjunction with something that no longer exists and with something that is still to come (or has yet to be completed). By taking into account the formal features of the relation, agents develop different temporal orientations towards the "no longer" and "not yet" depending on their goals and on what they expect or project, all of which are shaped by their past experiences. In order words, the present is experienced as being in flow. We hope that this line of reasoning clarifies the sense in which a decision-making process is a temporal issue. While the "I" speaks to itself in the present, it projects itself backwards and forwards in a temporal manner: the self (the "I" at T2) interprets the past self (the "me" at T1) to the future self (the "you" at T3). According to Vandenberghe (2014, 112), "[t]he upshot of this imaginary meeting of selves is a working consensus in which the conversational self tries to align context, concern and projects into a possible train of action". Pragmatism's legacy to this conception of decision making is obvious to the fact that it is approached as a "becoming" and not as a "being".

That "psychic systems" develop their own internal logic of processing external reality allows us to explore how people cope with the complexity and with the antinomies of their social relationships in which they live over the course of their lives. For this purpose, the researcher must study the experienced life history and the biographical stock of knowledge of the biographer obtained through his/her living in various social fields. Gender, class, ethnicity, locality and turning points occur in the family and participation in institutions or organizations is crucial to shaping the quality of biographical experiences. The stock of biographical experiences has not to do with fragmented and unconnected experiences that are collected by agents. On the contrary, it takes a peculiar, stratified and coherent form of Gestalt (Rosenthal 2018). It is within this stratified stock of knowledge that the implicit biographical knowledge is embedded, assuring the biographer that "he/she lives his/her own life", despite the inconsistencies faced. In addition, it constitutes the pre-reflective generative structure of people's biography, once every new event is turned into a biographical experience to the extent that it is incorporated into the already crystallized stock of biographical knowledge. Any new event, as soon as it is biographically appropriated, assumes new meaning according to the range of background knowledge and, at the same time, old experiences may be re-contextualized and re-evaluated in the light of new experiences.

Once people's biographies are embedded in relations in an ontological sense, it follows that what the researcher is investigating is the traces left by the emergent properties of these relations upon people's decisions. Humans are always and already engrossed in a historically structured field of social interactions and in a system of linguistically represented social classifications. This "socio-historical a priori" (Luckmann 1980) is what humans draw upon to make sense of their lives. Despite the fact that experiencing things is identified with subjects' capability of stating in the first person that "I did that..." or "I remember this...", reconstructing biographical experiences is not identical with a solipsistic and internal act of remembering, but is something that takes place in a public manner and in a collective context. Personal history meets and is inscribed into the histories of collectivities or histories of the "we". In order to construct biographical narrations, subjects select elements and cultural symbols from the socially shared stock of collective experiences and recollections (Halbwachs 1992). While in the moment of remembering, memory is always personal, with subjects recollecting and reconstructing their past as members of a social group. When subjects are called upon to talk about their life or to take decisions, they develop an internal dialogue by reviewing the relations in which they live, the relations they aspire to involve and the relations of which they are afraid. According to Archer (2015), these deliberations on the relations *per se* will influence the production of social phenomena in a qualitatively different way, generating a specific range of outcomes. Either seen as a "biographical code" or as "internal dialogue", agents' power of processing biographical experiences has a temporal grounding which is doubly formed: not only does a biographical construction as a generative structure give shape to biographical experiences, but it can be altered because of them (Alheit and Dausien 2000). Understanding how subjects process social reality as mediated through a crystallized biographical construction affords this process both a reproductive and a transformative dimension.

For CR, the cause of this morphogenetic/morphostatic process of which the outcomes are either reproductive or transformative lies in the relational goods or relational evils that have the power to motivate, inhibit or limit the parts composing the relation. When subjects deliberate, they do so in relation to those goods or evils issuing from the relation itself and not from the singulars of the relation. To remember what we analyzed in chapter 2, these goods and evils are properties of the relation and cannot be reduced to the lower-order properties of individuals because they are indivisible. They are relations' emergent powers that causally form subjects' biographies. "I do not want to let my parents down" or "I do not want to do what my parents want from me" are classic examples of relational goods or evils. In the first case, the emergent property is the commitment to a moral obligation, while in the second case, the emergent property is the rupture with it. A further example of where the temporal trace of a relation's form becomes apparent is Howard Becker's (1960) concept of a "side bet". In trying to explain why people remain committed to consistent lines of action even when better alternatives are offered, Becker maintains that the committed person has made a side bet in a previous temporal moment or a side bet in something else from which he/she cannot withdraw or cancel. In other words, one other (previous or simultaneous) side bet is so powerful that it commits subjects to remain consistent with a specific line of action, notwithstanding its deficiency or weakness.

Archer offers an example so as to illuminate the causal effects of relations' emergent properties. Consider the fictional scenario of a couple named David and Helen who are about to complete their postgraduate studies and want to retain their emotional bond after graduating. However, each of them has his/her own plans for after-graduation life. Archer is as opposed to rational action theorists who conceptualize decision making through game theoretic 2x2 tables as she is opposed to interpretivists who think that "empathy" is what enables Helen and David to commit to a common future because it fosters dialogue whereby each of them "gets into the shoes" of the other. Regarding the impasses of the interpretivist thesis, Archer (2015, 63) argues:

> However hard the two try, they produce Alter's interpretations of Ego's self-interpretations and vice versa, doing so *seriatim* with no way out of this trap. Goodwill on both sides cannot extricate them from it, meaning that hermeneutics cannot provide a secure basis for forging a life that captures what the two people value most.

Given that decision making has to negotiate with the question of "Where are they going to live after graduation?", David and Helen will reflect upon practical but crucial matters like the distance from their hometown or the cost of living. Nevertheless, these factors do not act as "push" variables. Such deliberation has to do with reflecting upon questions like "Where did we pass our best moments as a couple?", preparing their future life as a couple. Thus, "together" and "we" concern relational goods that have been developed throughout their common student life. In this case, "we-mode" thinking is an emergent phenomenon whereby both David and Helen refer to relational goods connected with memories in which they did things together. In the case that the most intense memory of this reflection is "walking in the countryside", it is possible that David and Helen will search for a house in a rural environment. Of course, reservations may emerge, such as Helen being afraid that she will lose some of her university friends or David being concerned that he has no driving license. In any case, it is the "relational goods" that shape the hierarchy of reservations or that provide the prism through which the couple will make sense of their options. However, it may be the case that this happy prospect is impossible to realize because Helen is too reluctant to lose her friends, in turn affecting her relationship with David.

Archer's example has the merit of underlining first the openness of "togetherness" in the face of future developments and second that the "we" is tied up with relational goods and evils that exist only on the condition that the "we" also exists. Should the "we" collapse, the relational goods will collapse, too. Nevertheless, what is not highlighted by Archer concerns the biographical grounding of the relation and we think that this point needs to be stressed because it is tied up with LMS. In particular, RBR has the power to identify the reasons why David and Helen are successful (or not) in continuing their common life as a couple after graduating and in creating a new household, by focusing on the biographical details of their stock of knowledge through which their "ultimate concerns" have been sedimented and upon which each of them articulates his/her "you". Such biographical research investigates the biographical transmutations of habitus in conjunction with the emergent properties of the relations they have lived (for example, university experiences). The merit of such research lies in pointing out the causal process through which necessary and sufficient conditions foster or inhibit David and Helen's encounter and in forging a causal hypothesis regarding the social phenomenon of "transition to adulthood of higher education students".

Regardless of how one conceives of "relational reflexivity", "biographical code" or "internal dialogue", the truth is that these should not be seen as an invocation of voluntarism, let alone of constructivist epistemology. On the contrary, this emphasis aims to underline the necessity of theorizing what is self-evident during a biographical interview, namely that subjects requested to reflect upon their lives converse both with the researcher and with their self. At the same time and by taking into consideration how LMS are formed, researchers implementing RBR want to explain how the things that pass unnoticed by the agents lead to specific (unintended) outcomes. In this way, subjects' reasoning takes priority without this leading to the traps of "psychologism" (psychological structures determine and explain actions) or "sociologism" (discourses give shape *ex nihilo* to motives). This is why we agree with Wengraf and Chamberlayne (2013) who, in commenting on the need to articulate a tenable theory of the subject for research purposes, state that biographical research should turn its attention to the social psychology of groups in order to understand the rapid social changes of our times. Beyond this, such a demand is directly related to the fact that whereas until the early 1990s Western societies' dominant orientation was the past or the routine, modern societies' vulnerabilities necessitate that people become more reflective regarding both the risks connected with them and the projects they aspire to realize.

It is well known that this reflexivity thesis is neither new nor without criticism (Spyridakis and Christodoulou 2019), especially regarding whether RBR can reconstruct and explain humans' LMS. First, there are those who argue that during the narrative interview,[2] a spurious and illusory linear and coherent life narration is constructed by the researcher with the effect that this narrative coherence is but an artefact. In this way, critics contend, biographical researchers treat interviewees as if they are persons with a stable and unifying source of expression through which an authentic and deep self emerges. Second, there are those who state that biographical researchers, searching for patterns stemming from people's biographies, impose upon the research material a kind of regularity and uniformity in order to explain it. In this way, they assume that a coherent core of self-identity exists from which life patterns come into play. This reservation can be answered as follows (Schäfer and Völter 2005): although the biographical self-presentation taking place in the communicative context of a biographical narrative interview can be seen as a performance aimed at constructing a self-image satisfying personal interests, it is not fully controlled by the interviewee. In particular, Schütze (1987) holds that interviewees, by trying to faithfully recall what they have lived and to depict the system of indexicalities related to their experiences, they are gradually engrossed into the flow of the narration, with the effect that the influences of the interview context and narrator's communicative strategies become minimized. In addition, the narrator's control over the end product of narration is limited, because in the second phase of the interview the interviewer asks follow-up questions about the initial part of the narrative. In this way, biographical researchers obtain a more accurate picture of events and experiences related to the narrator's past experiences and are able to bring to light whatever he/she did not mention, probably because it did not fit with the self-image he/she wanted to construct. By examining the above-mentioned criticisms through the lens of CR, one can trace radical constructivists' criticism to the fact that they have as their point of departure a flat ontology. On the contrary, the interrelations among narrated life stories, experienced life history and the generative mechanisms of the LMS are rendered interesting in so far as they are put in dialogue with CR's stratified social ontology. This is what we aspire to describe in detail in chapter 8.

Furthermore, the interpretation of texts produced through a biographical narrative interview reveals that life stories are neither linear nor coherent entities. Life stories take shape through contradictions, inconsistencies and discontinuities, entail various narrative pathways and must be analyzed as multi-voiced texts. Note that during an interview, what is communicated is not a ready-made biographical self-presentation and in this sense the interview process is not so much reproductive as it provides the narrator with the space to reflect, to contextualize anew and to re-construe his/her perspective in the face of his/her life history (Tsiolis 2006). This is why it is a "doing biography" process. Thus, a narrative interview does not promote a static and closed conception of self-identity. Rather, due to the historicity of the relations' forms and to the surplus of meaning that sustains life decisions, it prioritizes not only the morphostatic and reproductive but also the morphogenetic and transformative dimension of institutions and identities. It is this multiple process of reproduction and transformation that the biographical researcher must unravel.

Another line of criticism of RBR's claim to causation stems from radical constructivist epistemologies stating that even if one accepts that LMS exist, what remains unanswered pertains to how one can access them. A typical expression of this objection is made by Nassehi and Saake (2002), who argue that tracing into biographical self-presentation realities rooted not in texts but beyond is pointless and epistemologically untenable. Nassehi thinks that RBR has fallen into two epistemological traps due to disregarding the following distinctions. First is the distinction between "life course" and "biography". A "life course" is defined as the sum of events and turning points occurring in an individual's life, while a "biography" is defined as the "selective reproduction of life-events' selectivity" (Nassehi and Weber 1990, 161). A biography is "selective" because it does not take into account all of the events of a life course and it is a "selectivity" because this selection is contingent once it could take other forms. Biographies are the end product of observing life courses and at the same time these observations are independent of what really happened or was experienced because of the contingency of biography's possibilities as well as of the selective reconstructions of the past. Hence, biographies are not direct reproductions of the past but novel creations of an operational present. Seen as self-descriptions, quantitatively speaking they constitute simplifications of the self and qualitatively speaking they present a novel reality. In this sense they cannot provide any access to life courses (Jost 2005).

The second distinction Nassehi (1994) makes is between the biographical work of experiences that occur as a psychic process and thematizing life events that constitute a purely performative social operation. This distinction, Nassehi contends, renders Alheit and Dausien's (2000) conception of

biographies being self-referential structures issuing from psychically processing experiences untenable and futile. For Nassehi, biographical thematization is neither defined from the life history experienced nor a document
of the biographical appropriation of the social. Biographical thematizations
are solely and exclusively social performative operations, not psychic ones.
Biographical narration is the end product of a performance constructed in
the purely social interaction between the interviewer and the interviewee
and for this reason, whatever belongs to the psychic side of identity will
forever remain unknown and unknowable ("the dark side of the moon").

However, if Nassehi is right, what is the object of study from the perspective of biographical research? Nassehi (1994) responds that this object
may be biographical communication itself as well as its outcomes, meaning
the biographical texts. In any case, life courses, life histories or the psychic processing of experiences must be excluded as objects of biographical
research. Rather, research should focus on how the text is the final product
of reducing the contingencies that permeate it. Nassehi and Saake (2002,
81-82) hold that biographical researchers should focus "on how texts carry
the capacity of excluding other possibilities". Researchers should not search
for hidden meanings lying beneath the surface but bring to light the selectivity of the text[3] and the interactional or communicative strategies that enable
things to be presented in specific ways: "It is not the homology between life
and text that makes biographical narrations interesting but the contingency
and the unforeseeable character of their genesis" (Nassehi 1994, 59).

A first answer that can be given to the above radical constructivist-driven
criticisms and objections is that they do not take into consideration how
what really happened (the life course's life events) exists independently of
the narrator him/herself and affects causally how he/she makes sense of it.[4]
It is as if Nassehi and colleagues accept that what the researcher can access
is the present situation and the text stemming from it, while everything else
is either causally indifferent or unknowable. However, how are they certain
that not only are there no causal effects but that also they can never be
known? Their argument ends up accepting a kind of fragmented presentism
which is unable to theorize both the temporal nature of the social in non-
psychological terms and the conditions that make the performative character of the biographical construction possible. Furthermore, the absence of a
theory of the subject is striking.[5] The only conception of the subject implic-
itly sustaining Nassehi and colleagues' arguments concerns either a rational
actor or the manipulating self, like the one described by Goffman's theory.
However, for both of these theories of self, objections abound. Given that
we have analyzed in detail the deficiencies of the rational actor in chapter
3, let us say a few things about the dramaturgical self. How is one able to
manipulate audiences and act as a chameleon if one's mental entities and

reasons for action do not exist? Obviously, these reasons for action must preexist an actor's manipulations, because in a different case, performativity and dramaturgical performances have their cause not within a thinking subject but within a fragmented subject devoid of memory or recollections who plays out unconnected self-images in different situations. In this case, what we are talking about is not a divided self but a schizophrenic self. In contradistinction to this approach to the self, the argument we put forward in this book acknowledges, first, that subjects are capable of thinking and of doing things regardless of how rational their actions and, second, that we cannot eliminate the first-person perspective or the causal powers of human individuals from an explanation of human action. In this sense, we hold a realist view as far as humans' mental entities are concerned, in stark contrast with constructivists' anti-essentialist obsession that makes them unable to provide criteria as to whether when a house is burning, the first thing that needs to be saved is the computer or a human being. Alternatively, as Bunge (2006) has remarked regarding radical constructivists' delusion that there can be observations without things to observe, they are more interested in criticizing science than in defending it.

Finally, radical constructivists' glossocentrism is unable to theorize structure, in contrast to critical realism, the approach of which is much more open and non-deterministic. In particular, for critical realists, structures are framed as relations between positions that are ontologically discrete from agency, because they are temporal and emergent realities. Hence, instead of treating society as being composed of separate individuals who interact (as in symbolic interactionism), critical realists hold that the various defining features of social relations that need to be explained include social inequalities and the effects of the unequal distribution of resources. These issues are overlooked by the above-mentioned criticisms, while our argument, by combining RBR with CR, considers causal explanations a constitutive element of biographical research. Those who refuse to accept that social science's goal is to explain things which take place in social reality tend to identify causality with statistical explanation. However, what we propose in this book is exactly the opposite: that mechanism-based explanations can constitute the epistemological basis of biographical research. As we analyzed in the previous chapters, social mechanisms are not to be identified with "intervening variables" but should be seen as the unobservable causal path leading from a causal configuration to an outcome. In this line of reasoning, context matters, as it is within contexts that generative mechanisms emerge and it is social relations' openness that gives rise to social entities' powers to become activated. In short, mechanisms' outcomes depend upon context; they are not determined from some predefined linguistic or economic structure.

Notes

1 For Alheit and Dausien (2000, 264), "biographies present a structure of an outwardly oriented self-referentiality".
2 According to Schütze (1983), a narrative interview is organized in three phases: (a) the phase of main narration, in which the interviewee narrates his/her life in an extempore and impromptu way; (b) the phase of follow-up questions, in which the interviewer prompts the interviewee to continue his/her narration on issues interrupted in the first phase or to expand on issues that are unclear from it; and (c) the third phase, in which the interviewer asks questions about topics that remain unclear or asks the interviewee to evaluate or assess whatever he/she wants (see also Rosenthal 2018).
3 The selectivity that Nassehi and Saake discuss here is in stark contrast to what we considered in analyzing OH: in the former case, selectivity concerns the text, while in the latter, selectivity refers to how it structures the regularity of the case.
4 Wohlrab-Sahr (2002) notes regarding biographical narrations that despite the fact that the sequentiality of past biographical events takes the form of a text constructed in the present, the storied processes occurring within them and the way people have acted result in why the text has taken that form and not another.
5 Chamberlayne et al. (2000, 6) have made a similar argument as follows: "An extreme version of this postmodernist skepticism and refusal to make inferences from text were those who denied that actors had any coherent 'point of view' or any stable 'identity' that could be expressed by what they said or did".

References

Alheit, P. "Identität oder "Biographizität"? Beiträge der neueren sozial- und erziehungswissenschaftlichen Biographieforschung zu einem Konzept der Identitätsentwicklung." In *Subjekt – Identität – Person? Reflexionen zur Biographieforschung*, edited by P. Griese, 219–49. Wiesbaden: VS Verlag, 2010.
Alheit, P., and B. Dausien. "Die biographische Konstruktion der Wirklichkeit. Überlegungen zur Biographizität des Sozialen." In *Biographische Sozialisation*, edited by E. Hoerning, 257–83. Stuttgart: Lucius & Lucius, 2000.
Archer, M. "The Relational Subject and the Person: Self, Agent, and Actor." In *The Relational Subject*, edited by P. Donati, and M. Archer, 85–123. Cambridge: Cambridge University Press, 2015.
Becker, S.H. "Notes on the Concept of Commitment." *American Journal of Sociology* 66, no. 1 (1960): 32–40. doi:10.1086/222820.
Bude, H. *Deutsche Karrieren*. Frankfurt/M.: Suhrkamp, 1987.
Bude, H. "Lebenskonstruktionen als Gegenstand der Biographieforschung." In *Biographische Methoden in Den Humanwissenschaften*, edited by G. Jüttemann, and H. Thomae, 247–58. Weinheim: Beltz, 1998.
Bunge, M. *Chasing Reality: Strife over Realism*. Toronto: University of Toronto Press, 2006.
Chamberlayne, P., J. Bornat, and T. Wengraf. *The Turn to Biographical Methods in Social Science*. London and New York: Routledge, 2000.

Halbwachs, M. *On Collective Memory*. Chicago and London: The University of Chicago Press, 1992.

Jost, G. "Radikaler Konstruktivismus – ein Potenzial für die Biographieforschung." In *Biographieforschung im Diskurs*, edited by B. Völter, B. Dausien, H. Lutz, and G. Rosenthal, 213–27. Wiesbaden: VS Verlag, 2005.

Luckmann, T. *Lebenswelt und Gesellschaft. Grundstrukturen und geschichtliche Wandlungen*. München-Wien-Zürich: Paderborn, 1980.

Nassehi, A. "Die Form der Biographie. Theoretische Überlegungen zur Biographieforschung in methodologischer Absicht." *Bios - Zeitschrift für Biographieforschung & Oral History* 7 (1994): 46–63.

Nassehi, A., and G. Weber. "Zur einer Theorie biographischer Identität. Epistemologische und systemtheoretische Argumente." *Bios - Zeitschrift für Biographieforschung & Oral History* 2 (1990): 153–87.

Nassehi, A., and I. Saake. "Kontingenz: Methodisch verhindert oder beobachtet? Ein Beitrag zur Methodologie der qualitativen Sozialforschung." *Zeitschrift für Soziologie* 31, no. 1 (2002): 66–86. doi:10.1515/zfsoz-2002-0104.

Rosenthal, G. *Interpretive Social Research*. Göttingen: Göttingen University Press, 2018.

Sawyer, R.K. *Social Emergence. Societies as Complex Systems*. Cambridge: Cambridge University Press, 2005.

Schäfer, T., and B. Völter. "Subjekt-Positionen. Michel Foucault und die Biographieforschung." In *Biographieforschung im Diskurs*, edited by B. Völter, B. Dausien, H. Lutz, and G. Rosenthal, 161–88. Wiesbaden: VS Verlag, 2005.

Schütze, F. "Biographieforschung und Narratives Interview." *Neue Praxis* 13 (1983): 283–93.

Schütze, F. *Das narrative Interview in Interaktionsfeldstudien. Teil I*. Studienbrief der Fernuniversität in Hagen, Hagen, 1987.

Spyridakis, M., and M. Christodoulou. "The Life-Course Determinants of Falling from Grace: On the Temporalities of Precariousness." In *Emotions, Temporalities and Working-Class Identities in the 21st Century*, edited by M. Christodoulou, and M. Spyridakis, 43–73. New York: Nova Press Publishers, 2019.

Tsiolis, G. *Life Stories and Biographical Narrations. Biographical Approach in Sociological Qualitative Research*. Athens: Kritiki (in Greek), 2006.

Vandenberghe, F. *What's Critical About Critical Realism? Essays in Reconstructive Social Theory*. London and New York: Routledge, 2014.

Wengraf, T., and P. Chamberlayne. "Biography-Using Research (BNIM), SOSTRIS, Institutional Regimes and Critical Psychosocietal Realism." In *Realist Biography and European Policy*, edited by J. Turk, and A. Mrozowicki, 63–92. Leuven: Leuven University Press, 2013.

Wohlrab-Sahr, M. "Prozessstrukturen, Lebenskonstruktionen, biographische Diskurse. Positionen im Feld soziologischer Biographieforschung und mögliche Anschlüsse nach außen." *BIOS - Zeitschrift für Biographieforschung & Oral History* 1 (2002): 3–23.

8 Case reconstruction and relational mechanisms in biographical research practice

Although one of the goals of the book is to clarify the sense in which reconstructive biographical approach and critical realism (CR) constitute the main philosophical and theoretical principles of a unifying framework for biographical research practice, one has to keep in mind their main difference: reconstructive biographical research (RBR) offers a theoretical and methodological framework for practising biographical research while CR is a meta-theoretical and philosophical tradition proposing specific socio-ontological and epistemological ideas. This means that whereas (RBR) has developed specific methodological tools for analyzing biographical material, this is not the case for CR. We have to note that fertile attempts have been made to delineate how CR can be methodologically implemented as a coding procedure. However, these attempts use elements of grounded theory's methodology, which is based on fragmenting the transcribed text so that thematic codes can be inductively generated. By contrast, RBR uses transcribed texts as a whole but without clearly showing how one can claim causality by analyzing biographical narratives. For this reason, we have drawn upon a process tracing approach in order to fill this gap because, as we showed in chapter 3, doing so enables us to merge the CR-inspired concept of "relational mechanisms" with the latent meaning structures (LMS) of RBR. We argue that the process tracing approach to causality and RBR are compatible under the philosophical ideas on causality propounded by CR. This is what we demonstrate in this chapter, namely how RBR can be methodologically implemented through the lens of process tracing causality and relational generative mechanisms.

Before we proceed to the details of our argumentation, let us summarize the main conclusions reached in the two previous chapters.

- The key for the identification of LMS is the examination of how agents make choices and not-choices throughout their life course (the "selectivity processes" we referred to in chapter 6);

- To this end, one has to research the sequential structure of the forms of social relations from which agents pass and the social nexuses of which they are a part;
- Generative mechanisms have their roots in these forms and in the peculiarity of agents' biographical temporality;
- LMS are the traces left by these relational mechanisms

Gabrielle Rosenthal (2018) has provided specific propositions regarding the temporal structuring of life histories and the present biographical constructions, which we believe provide a perfect starting point for the identification of the relational mechanisms. She proposes two principles that are related a) to the necessity of taking into account how social phenomena are formed, reproduced and transformed (this resembles the morphostatic and morphogenetic dynamic of the social proposed by Archer) and b) to the necessity of taking into account how past temporal frameworks of meaning making are connected to present ones. In particular, Rosenthal (2018, 159-160) holds that

A. In order to understand and explain social and psychological phenomena we have to reconstruct their genesis: the process of their creation, reproduction and transformation.
B. In order to understand and explain people's actions, one should not stop at analyzing subjects' point of view but also their courses of action. We want to find out what they experienced, what meaning they gave their actions at the time, what meaning they assign today and in what biographically constituted context they place their experiences.
C. In order to understand and explain the statements made by interviewees/biographers concerning particular topics or experiences in their past, it is necessary to interpret the latter as part of the overall context of their current life and their present and future perspectives.

These three principles can be set in motion methodologically through the following four practices:

(a) the procedure of case reconstruction;
(b) the sequential analysis;
(c) the abductive inference process; and
(d) the analytic distinction between the experienced life history and the narrated life story.

In the following paragraphs we provide details for each of them.

The procedure of case reconstruction

This is a distinguishing feature of RBR because it encourages researchers to approach every case as a whole and as the crystallization of a genetical process. The assumption sustaining this process is that there exists a unifying principle shaping agents' biographical Gestalt through specific rules. Gestalt's part obtains meaning by means of its relation to the whole Gestalt and to the rules of its structuring. Thus, interpreting each case is to reconstruct the rules of its structuring and to discover how Gestalt's parts are interconnected. The principle of case reconstruction runs counter to separating or fragmenting various parts of the text and then subsuming them under predefined theoretical categories and classifications (Rosenthal 2018, 50). The rationale of "subsumption" is that the parts of the whole have a stable and autonomous meaning that should not be related to the whole structure of the case. According to case reconstruction's principles, a life event obtains a meaning according to how it is inscribed in the totality of the structure of each particular life history. Recalling what we analyzed in the previous two chapters, each biographical event can be reconstructed only if one investigates how it is positioned within the sequentiality of previous and subsequent biographical experiences and how it is processed through the LMS that permeate the agent's biography.

The sequential analysis

To the extent that each case's structure is not a static entity but a process of becoming, it follows that its hermeneutic reconstruction has to take into account the sequential pattern of its constitutive elements. In addition, once the text is conceived of as the objectified form – as a protocol – of social reality, the analysis has to be based on this sequential articulation of the text. Thus, assembling the text's parts in discordance to this articulation should be avoided. The principle of sequential analysis necessitates, first, to investigate the text's parts in relation to their sequence and, second, to state clearly all the possible ways of interpreting a part before the researcher moves to the next part (Oevermann et al. 1979). Bruno Hildenbrand (1987, 154) notes that in analyzing a sequential structure, it matters how "each text is interpreted step by step without the researcher anticipating what follows", in the sense that the researcher has to put in brackets his/her preconceptions about the text in order to exhaust in a persistent, systematic and disciplined manner all the hermeneutic possibilities stemming from one specific part of it. By contrast, when the researcher interprets a text unit by making use of the next part of the text, he/she risks not covering all the hermeneutic possibilities and naively adopting the biographer's perspective. In such a case, the outcome is not case reconstruction but re-telling what the biographer said. Reconstructing the importance of a text unit is tied up with creating the inner context of the next text unit. The researcher analyzes each text unit by mentally experimenting with all the possible versions of how it will proceed. Then, the researcher examines the selected version by contrasting it with the range of all the remaining hermeneutic possibilities. In this way, the peculiar selectivity process is gradually evolved through which this specific case is structured and is made unique. In other words, what is evolved concerns the peculiar logic through which specific choices are made while other possibilities are avoided. Seen through this angle, the text is nothing but a protocol of a transformation process (Wernet 2000).

The abductive inference process

As we noted previously, mental experimentation is central to RBR analysis and its goal is to disengage the analyzed text unit from all its real internal and external contexts so that alternative hermeneutic possibilities can be proposed by inventing different contexts and alternative readings. The contrast between all these possibilities and what is adopted leads, in parallel with sequential analysis, to the reconstruction of a case's structure. Through this multi-level and sequential analysis of eliminating alternatives, the ultimate goal is to bring to light how this structure is sustained by means of its peculiar selectivity process. It has been noted by many scholars that this analytic procedure resembles Peirce's abductive reasoning, an example of which is offered by how Sherlock Holmes uncovers crimes (Rosenthal 2018). The detective Holmes deals with cases in a manner quite different from that of the police, who pose a hypothesis ("the brother is the murderer") and search for indices supporting it ("the brother has no alibi, his/her fight with the victim last night, they had financial issues"). By contrast, Holmes proceeds in an abductive way by starting from the observables ("the victim's room was locked and the window broken") and tries to gather all the possible ways of interpreting them ("the broken window might be connected with how the murderer got into the room, with his/her exit from it or with both of these options, or it may have to do with a fake entrance to the room"). Then, the detective tries to infer the various and contrastive connotations stemming from each of these understandings ("what would be the direction of the broken glass and the situation of the flowerpot in the case that the window was broken by someone inside the room in contrast to outside of it?"). At this point, the findings ("the location of the broken glass and the situation of the flowerpot") are investigated as indices that corroborate or disprove these contrastive understandings.

This kind of data analysis comprises three steps: a) by starting from something observable, the researcher states all the possible interpretations of the phenomenon; b) all the relevant consequences stemming from these interpretations are drawn from the researcher who poses specific hypotheses for each of them and counterfactually examines their sustainability; and c) by taking into account all these hypotheses, the researcher examines the findings that verify them (or not). The interpretation that cannot be eliminated through this process should be deemed the most appropriate. Abductive reasoning is at the heart of how RBR analyzes cases because it requires the researcher to put forward hypotheses by starting from the text itself and not by subsuming it to predefined categories. At the same time, it prompts researchers to check the viability of his/her informed guesses. However, we have to stress that abduction should be seen neither as a mere descriptive tool nor as something based solely on a researcher's charisma. On the contrary, researchers have to be theoretically prepared in order to interpret the text and to become engaged with the conceptual schemes of the scientific field in which the phenomenon of interest is inscribed and with the relevant literature so as to be sensitized. As we indicated in chapter 5, abduction and retroduction in CR involve theoretically redescribing a phenomenon of interest and identifying mechanisms that may account for it and how they behave. Thus, by implementing creative dialogue between data and theoretical ideas, researchers are able to make sophisticated guesses, to highlight possible connections of seemingly unrelated findings and to produce interesting causal hypotheses.

The analytic distinction between the experienced life history and the narrated life story

This distinction between the "experienced life history" and the "narrated life story" has been proposed by Rosenthal and concerns a) the biographer's perspective of the past at the time the events took place (the "then") and b) his/her present perspective at the time of his/her narration (the "now") (Rosenthal 2018). Regarding the "then" of the past present, by following the principles of case reconstruction and of sequential analysis, researchers try to reconstruct the most crucial dimensions of a person's biographical experience and of their sedimented biographical stock of knowledge. This reconstruction is focused on their "then" perspective concerning how the person had lived a state of affairs in the past and on identifying their actions' orientation at the past moment when they took place. To this end, researchers must be sensitive to the contextual factors within which the biographical experience was shaped (Donati and Archer 2015). The researcher approaches in a sequential way each distinct period of experienced life history by stating hypotheses regarding:

- elements around which biographers build their self-image;
- how they make sense of their social position and of their capacities to act;
- how they articulate and connect their important life events and their attitude towards them;
- their biographical orientations and plans as well as their fulfilment or not;
- their biographically sedimented action strategies and the nexus of values they adopt; and
- their web of relationships with significant others around which their sense of belonging is formed.

Analyzing an action within the flow of the experienced life history – the action as it is positioned within the temporal sequence of the biographer's significant events – has the advantage of taking into account its specific social or other contexts. Researchers can mentally reconstruct an action's contexts, the possibilities offered to subjects and the preferred action patterns that fit these contexts. In addition, researchers may: a) interpret an action's orientation from his/her own point of view by focusing on his/her modes of action as they are crystallized into his/her biographically sedimented stock of knowledge; and b) assess the intended and the unintended consequences of the action. Hence, the act of reconstructing is not limited to decoding a biographer's manifest meanings but aspires to identify the latent meaning produced as much when the action took place in the past as when the action is analyzed from the "now" of the narration. In addition, the researcher can decode how biographers are oriented towards the grammar of the socially offered action patterns and how they position their self when confronted with the obstacles and the opportunities offered by the conditions in which they live (what are the options offered, how biographers make sense of them and what are the decisions taken).

Besides social action, analyzing biographical narratives affords privileged access to biographical experience. Experience, for Fischer and Kohli (1987), entails a twofold temporal horizon composed of the past and the future: past experiences, sedimented as biographical knowledge, provide biographers with a spectrum of expectations that function as matrices for novel experience. In addition, past experiences may be re-interpreted and approached under a new prism owing to subsequent critical biographical moments. New experiences either confirm or transform biographical knowledge, leading to a re-interpretation of past experiences. In this way, an *ex post* re-evaluation of various aspects of a biographer's stock of knowledge may lead to a further stratification of biographical experiences. Researchers, by capitalizing on an experience's temporal sequentiality, which is depicted in the text of biographical self-thematization, may reconstruct through mental experimentation how biographers perceive of various events in the "then" (the past present), that is, within the "then" biographical layer of knowledge. Researchers may consequently analyze the dialectical relation developed between the biographical knowledge and the new experiences derived from both of these perspectives: both from how the "then" sedimented biographical knowledge operates as the matrix for processing a new experience and from how this new experience confirms or transforms the main axes of biographical orientation. Subsequently, researchers may forge hypotheses regarding the development and the transmutation of these biographical axes within biographers' temporal flow and interpret the biographical transitions that took place over the life course because of the peculiar way social changes are inscribed within their personal life. In other words, they may analyze how a specific biography has been constructed through its specific appropriation of the social reality and within a specific historical and social context.

Finally, analyzing actions and experiences within the different biographical periods of the experienced life history enables researchers to craft hypotheses regarding the nexus of patterns characterizing biographers' action strategies and orientations. In this way, researchers can trace the distinctive LMS for each biography, that is, the peculiar nexus of rules, practices and meanings upon which life is grounded.

Let us now turn to the analysis of the narrated life story that focuses on how biographies are constructed by biographers' present perspective (in the "now"): how "we live our past in the present" (Fischer-Rosenthal and Rosenthal 1997, 148) and "in what way a person articulates his experiences and makes them a substantial part of his/her biography" (Dausien 1996, 109). The assumption is that biographical experiences are not considered as objects contained within a biographer's stock of knowledge and classified in a static manner ready to be recalled as if they refer to events "as they really took place". Rather, biographical experiences are re-evaluated depending on the present perspective and in the light of new situations. This does not mean that the way the biographer stands towards his/her biography is arbitrary or the product of a coincidence, but rather is based as much on his/her individually experienced life history as on the stories of the "we" to which he/she is related. As Fischer-Rosenthal and Rosenthal (1997) note, narrated life stories refer not only to how one is related to his/her past in the present but also to the "then" experiencing of these past experiences. However, the relation between the life as "then" lived and the life as "now" is told not in terms of correspondence (Rosenthal 1995) but as multi-layered dialogue open to transformations.

The importance of the present perspective and its influence on the creation of biographical self-presentation has been acknowledged by Peter Alheit (1990), who considers narration as an "as if" action. According to Alheit, biographers through narration are transformed into "as if" actors who transpose their selves into the position of the actor within the past situation. The narrator has to recall the context of the experience as well as the actor's way of thinking and preferred action strategies. In this way, the narrator connects the flow of his/her narration with what he/she has experienced. However, he/she is moving constantly between various temporal perspectives: from the present point of the narrative act, the narrator recalls the (previous for the narrator) present of the actor in the face of an anticipated future for the actor (but one that is past for the narrator). The narrator applies an order to the sequence of past events by knowing their development and their subsequent causal relations. Within the context of a long narration, the narrator reconstructs causally and temporally his/her experiences and actions and makes up a coherent whole. Thus he/she positions him/herself towards a specific past experience by having an implicit or explicit stance regarding its relevance for the development of his/her life history. The meaning attached to the past event at the moment of the narration, even though it refers to the meaning it had at the moment the event took place, cannot be exactly the same as at that time, instead of being framed from the present perspective of the narrator who reconstructs the event through its connection with the subsequent events and with its importance to his/her life history. Furthermore, the selection of the events and of the experiences that are selected for narration depends on where the present perspective turns its attention. Thus, biographical narration always entails the process of reconstruction.

From this analysis it follows that every biographical narration capitalizing on the interconnectedness between narration and temporality thematizes the self in process, as something that is evolved and not as a static entity. Biographical narration presents the self in relation to all the relevant biographical transformations. Instead of emphasizing a static self-image, a biographical exposition prioritizes how the self has become what it is in time. Each extempore narration is a retrospective perspective on the transformations and developments of the narrator's self as the bearer of the biography (Schütze 1987). Recapitulating a person's biographical trajectory from his/her own perspective enables "the changing attitude of the biographer towards him/herself and his/her biography" to come to light (Dausien 1996, 108).

Researchers have to analyze the narrated life story and focus on the thematic and temporal articulation of the text units and on the selected kind of genre used for this emplotment (narration, argumentation and description). They have to reconstruct "the rules underlying the genesis of the biographical narration presented in the present of the interview, or, in more general terms, the self-presentation" (Rosenthal 2018, 175).

It is important at this point to highlight the connectedness that exists between the levels of the RBR analysis we referred to before and the three-level social ontology of CR. A more accurate picture of this connection is depicted in the following figure.

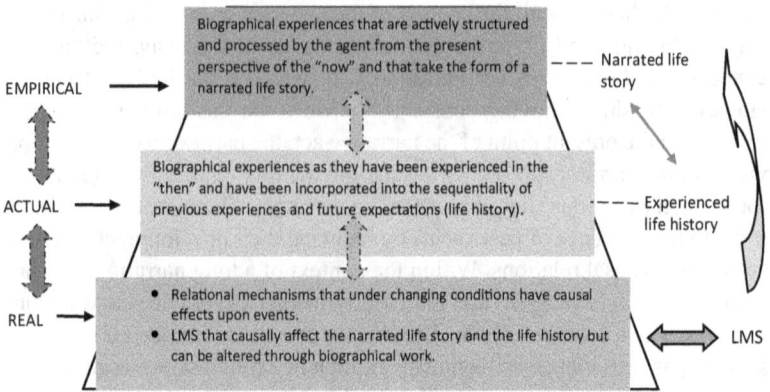

Figure 8.1 Depiction of merging RBR approach with CR three-level ontology.

The aim of the above scheme is to identify how LMS, experienced life history and narrated life story are related to the three-level ontology of CR in a non-mechanical way. We have put LMS at the level of the real because they can function as generative mechanisms as far as action, decision making and experiencing life experiences are concerned. LMS as generative structures give shape to biographical experiences, but it can be altered because of them. What needs to be stressed is that LMS are historically and socially formed because they are tied up with a narrator's biographical Gestalt, in which various life experiences are crystallized via his/her passing through various historical, social and cultural contexts (Alheit 2010). This is depicted by the blue arrow connecting LMS with experienced life history: LMS are embedded in experienced life history and at the same time they frame how external influences (events) are mediated through their logic by transforming them into biographical experiences and actions. Elements of both LMS and experienced life history are at the disposal of agents, but neither all the time nor in their whole range, in the sense that they become noticed through narrative thematization; that is, as narrated life story, meaning that they pass at the empirical level. In this way, experienced life history and narrated life story do not correspond mechanically to the actual and the empirical, respectively, while their multiple mediations are highlighted (see also Rosenthal 1995).

Both narrated life story and experienced life history[1] can offer researchers access to the various social relations from which agents have passed and consequently to the conditions within which specific relational mechanisms have been acted out. Despite the fact that it is human agents who produce structures of meaning, these structures become latent exactly because agents are always with others. Thus, in saying that biographical research deals with people's lived experiences, one has to make the addition that experiences are social products because "they are not simply a set of sense-data, but rather the result of our application of a socially influenced conceptual framework to the interpretation of that sense data" (Elder-Vass 2007, 179). Therefore, events taking place in the actual level that have been experienced as life history by the agents are selectively perceived by them. Despite its selectivity regarding the perception of the event, agents' intentionality – reconstructed as life story – affords us access through LMS to the deeper ontological level of the real, in which relational mechanisms are acted out. We think that according to this downwardly inclusive view of explaining events (as Elder-Vass calls it), RBR brings to light the interaction that exists between these three levels by highlighting how social forms' relational properties affect LMS. In any case, we need to explore lower-level configurations to make sense of the extent and the nature of the wild disjunction of multiple realizability, i.e. cases where the higher-level outcome is consistent with a variety of lower-level configurations.

Furthermore, in our view the relational mechanisms are neither static nor work one-sidedly. Both CR and RBR acknowledge agency in a non-voluntarist way: for CR, agents' reasons for action are causally effective and their life choices are not solely the result of habitual thinking but of reflexive deliberation, while for RBR, actions are mediated through agents' biographical intake. This means that relational mechanisms are open to change exactly because of both society's and biography's openness and of the fact that the outcome(s) of being with others cannot be predicted. This is where one of most important contributions of biographical research and especially of RBR lies, namely the explanation and understanding of social change. Donati (2011) thinks that understanding social change is to explore the differences between "before and after" (time registers) in successions or passages from one condition of a social entity to another. There are three such types of registers of time that sustain social entities' transformation: the event time of the interactional register of the micro level, the historic time of the relational register of the meso level and the symbolic dilated-timeout-of-time register of the macro level. For example, the social phenomenon of prolonging the duration of university studies for most contemporary young adults has to be examined through all three registers of time, as interactions are embedded in social relations, whose forms present properties that are directly related to how universities organize their social time, for example the duration of undergraduate or postgraduate studies, the assigning of work hours according to the European Credit Transfer System (ECTS) to university courses, or the entry of digital technologies into the act of teaching. As Donati (2011) argues, the identity of a social form must be seen as an "overlapping" between the three registers. A social form can be considered as a configuration that assumes a variety of relations between the three registers and can be said to be constituted by order and variety. We hold that RBR can highlight the varieties of social time that present most of the social phenomena by investigating the interconnectedness between people's biographical temporality and social relations' temporal form. In this sense, contingency presents modalities depending on the peculiar relational properties that emerge in social relations. By researching biographical temporalities, RBR enables access to the temporal form of social relations from which agents have passed throughout their lives.

Note

1 To analyze experienced life history, the researcher makes use of the elements contained within the narrated life story. In addition, he/she could rely on other sources, like documents or interviews with other family members, or historical or socio-political data relevant to the case at hand (Rosenthal 2018).

References

Alheit, P. *Alltag und Biographie. Studien zur gesellschaftlichen Konstitution biographischer Perspektiven.* Bremen: Universität Bremen, 1990.

Alheit, P. "Identität oder "Biographizität"? Beiträge der neueren sozial- und erziehungswissenschaftlichen Biographieforschung zu einem Konzept der Identitätsentwicklung." In *Subjekt – Identität – Person? Reflexionen zur Biographieforschung*, edited by B. Griese, 219–49. Wiesbaden: VS Verlag, 2010.

Dausien, B. *Biographie und Geschlecht.* Bremen: Donat Verlag, 1996.

Donati, P. *Relational Sociology. A New Paradigm for the Social Sciences.* London and New York: Routledge, 2011.

Donati, P., and M. Archer. "Introduction: Relational Sociology: Reflexive and Realist." In *The Relational Subject*, edited by P. Donati, and M. Archer, 3–33. Cambridge: Cambridge University Press, 2015.

Elder-Vass, D. "Re-Examining Bhaskar's Three Ontological Domains. The Lessons from Emergence." In *Contributions to Social Ontology*, edited by C. Lawson, J. Latsis, and N. Martins, 160–77. London and New York: Routledge, 2007.

Fischer, W., and M. Kohli. "Biographieforschung." In *Methoden der Biographie- und Lebenslaufforschung*, edited by W. Voges, 25–49. Opladen: Leske + Budrich, 1987.

Fischer-Rosenthal, W., and G. Rosenthal. "Narrationsanalyse Biographischer Selbstpräsentation." In *Sozialwissenschaftliche Hermeneutik*, edited by R. Hitzler, and A. Honer, 133–65. Opladen: Leske + Budrich, 1997.

Hildenbrand, B. "Wer soll bemerken, dass Bernard krank wird? Familiale Wirklichkeitskonstruktionsprozesse bei der Erstmanifestation einer schizophrenen Psychose." In *Zugänge zur Sicht des Subjektes mittels qualitativer Forschung*, edited by J. Bergold, and U. Flick. Tübingen: DGVT-Verlag, 151–62, 1987.

Oevermann, U., T. Allert, E. Konau, and J. Krambeck. "Die Methodologie einer «Objektiven Hermeneutik» und ihre allgemeinforschungslogische Bedeutung in den Sozialwissenschaften." In *Interpretative Verfahren in den Sozial- und Textwissenschaft*, edited by H.-G. Brose, 352–434. Stuttgart: Metzler, 1979.

Rosenthal, G. *Erlebte und erzählte Lebensgeschichte*. Frankfurt/M: Campus, 1995.

Rosenthal, G. *Interpretive Social Research*. Göttingen: Göttingen University Press, 2018.

Schütze, F. *Das narrative Interview in Interaktionsfeldstudien*. Teil I. Studienbrief der Fernuniversität in Hagen, 1987.

Wernet, A. *Einführung in die Interpretationstechnik der Objektiven Hermeneutik*. Opladen: Leske + Budrich, 2000.

9 Epilogue
Summarizing the argumentation

In this book, we have defended the view that biographical research should constitute an extremely valuable tool for attaining causal explanations for social phenomena. We have advanced an argumentation for how one can claim mechanism-based explanations by means of biographical research. The importance of establishing mechanism-based explanations lies in the fact that by identifying mechanisms, one can establish that a causal relation is at work; moreover, mechanisms eliminate the possibility of confounding spurious with real causes (Steel 2004). We are aware that the realization of such a goal presupposes specific arguments regarding contested and intractable philosophical and theoretical disputes. We have picked up as the main philosophical issue the following: to the extent that social causation can be achieved via biographical methods, what is the conception of causality upon which this argument rests? In this book, we have proposed the idea that mechanism-based explanations can be of use to biographical researchers, but this is an overly general and unspecified statement for our argument to be taken seriously. For this reason, we have been compelled to articulate a clear line of reasoning regarding both how we conceive of social mechanisms and what is our stance against the mechanism-based explanations that are widely used in qualitative research. This is why we considered that it was important to discuss at length in the first chapter the shortcomings of a dominant philosophical current that approaches mechanistic explanations through the prism of ontological and methodological individualism.

We believe that ontological and methodological individualists' main deficiency concerns their use of social wholes for explanatory reasons without providing a sufficient theoretical framing of them or without acknowledging their causal efficiency. In particular, individualists try to make sense of the irreducibility of the social through the multiple realization argument. The problem is that whenever such an argument is put into practice without the addition of wild disjunction, social wholes or social concepts (social roles, relations, organizations) are presupposed in the descriptions of individualists without the elimination of holistic concepts. In chapter 2 we clarified the reasons why the response to the deficiencies of the reductionism adopted by individualists is, the stratified ontology of emergentism, seen as non-reductive individualism. Non-reductive emergentism describes cases in which lower-level parts interact in ways that the upper-level configurations formed present irreducible and causally effective properties. Two of the most comprehensively discussed features of these higher-level properties are their novelty and their non-predictability. What is crucial in this idea is that a large proportion of social phenomena related to the unintended consequences of actions owe their existence not to actors' rationality or reasons for action but to the causal power of these emergent properties of the whole. Therefore, emergence stands in stark contrast to reductionist explanations, which tend to reduce upper-level phenomena to mere knowledge of their parts. Second, these emergent properties bear causal power independent of the constituents of the interacting parts and with the potential to shape their action. This view is opposed to the reductionist views espoused by methodological individualists who do not deny the existence of collectives, but believe that their explanations should be reduced to individual properties, be they psychological dispositions or individuals' reasons for action. In other words, in this kind of reductionism, the macro is explained in terms of micro properties.

The emergentist way of explaining social phenomena is compatible with case studies and biographical research, where explanation can be singular once it is unnecessary for an explanation to be subsumed under a generalizable law. In contrast with the abovementioned micro-foundation approach in which relational properties' causal efficacy is denied, the non-reductive emergentist perspective is consistent with emergent social properties that have causal power. The argument of non-reductive individualism is complemented by the philosophical arguments of supervenience, of multiple realization and of wild disjunction, which hold that the relation between emergent social properties and their realizing mechanisms is one of token identity but not of type identity. Remember that token identity means that two events can be causally related always within spatiotemporally located conditions. Supervenience is composed of two interconnected ideas: first, that if two events are identical with respect to their description at the lower level, then they do not differ at the higher level; and second, that an entity cannot change at a higher level without also changing at the lower level. However, as the arguments which denote the unpredictability and the novelty of each level (Kim 1999; Bunge 2009) have shown, supervenience is not a solution because it cannot sustain the causal power of higher-level entities. Similarly, Sawyer (2005) argues that supervenience presupposes ontological individualism but not methodological reductionism. At this point, the argument of multiple realization comes into play. In order to deal with the unpredictability of higher-level properties, individualists have made use of the multiple realizability argument. In simple terms this means that, although supervenient, each token instance of any social property can be realized by a different individual property. At the social level this means that the same reasons for action can give rise to different social wholes. In other words, on any token occasion, a social property must be realized by a mechanism involving its individual components but on different occasions, the same social property may be realized by different mechanisms (multiple realizability) and these different mechanisms may not be similar in any sociologically meaningful way (wild disjunction). The concept of wild disjunction demonstrates that a social property may be realized in highly inconsistent social fields through different relational mechanisms.

We think that this analysis enables the reader to understand why mechanism-based explanations fit with qualitative research and in particular with biographical research: first, because causality in qualitative research tends to be singular – that is, "case specific" – without this meaning that the explanatory propositions drawn from it are unamenable to generalization; and second, because the level at which the mechanisms are to be detected is not belief formation or social situations but the configurational structure permeating the parts of higher-order entities. Biographical research is a way of explaining social phenomena not as types but as tokens; that is, as particular and specific events localized in time and space. By approaching social events as tokens, the explanation occurs case by case and the causality is singular. Causality is singular when one identifies the specific conditions that mediate between an antecedent and a consequent event. In this case we are not considering what is called "invariable succession" between two types of events, one of which is the cause and the other is the effect, but rather with tracing the anterior conditions triggering relational processes through which a given result occurs. What matters in this causal reasoning is the identification of the conditions that make the difference. The cause changes the course of events in the sense that had it not existed, then a divergent course of events would have occurred. In other words, the absence of the cause would have been followed by a divergent course of events. According to this counterfactual thinking, the results would have been different had the cause not occurred. Although this counterfactually conceived singular causality is not holistic, we regard it as a powerful explanatory tool because it prioritizes the identification of the particular causal process leading from the antecedent event A to the subsequent event B and not C by taking into account the causal field enabling them.

Up to this point we have shown why singular causality suits mechanism-based explanations of social phenomena through the use of biographical research, without adopting the reductionism to which individualistic conceptions of causality lead. The next step of our argument lies in clarifying what it means for mechanisms to be found at the configurational level of social relations, or that mechanisms are relational. The arguments of Sawyer (2004) and Donati (2015) are useful for us because they point to the fact that the concept of wild disjunction is related to the existence of non-reducible properties of the relations' forms. Donati's relational realism complements in a socio-theoretical sense these philosophical ideas. Donati's relational perspective is Simmelian in many respects. He notes that social facts are constituted by social relations, the processual structure of which characterizes the emergence of every social form. Although friendship presupposes two or more people contributing to its existence, it entails assumptions that do not depend on them and involves things that go beyond their individuality. This implies a togetherness (a "we-relationship") that calls into play more than the friends' own individuality. As a consequence, Donati's contribution lies in proposing a non-nominalist conception of the relation that stands in stark contrast to both "conflationist" and "aggregativity-inspired" conceptions of relationality. The task of relational sociology is to analyze the process through which this structure of interdependence is generated, reproduces itself and changes. Knowing a social relation means being able to identify its "We-relation" properties, not simply interpreting how each separate individual makes sense of another. Donati proposes the idea that besides or in addition to the distinct contributions of the ego and the alter to the relation, relationality as such presents its own contribution as well. In grounding our argument in a critical-realist inspired relational sociology, we highlighted the relational, processual and transformative character of "lived experience" as well as the relational constitution of biographical constructions.

One of the central themes of the book is that the abovementioned arguments of relational social ontology intersect with the theoretical grounds of reconstructive biographical research (RBR). We have summarized these theoretical commonalities in the following ideas:

- Both critical realism and RBR claim that causal explanations should be a major goal of social research;
- The three-level social ontology of CR can function as a frame for conceptualizing latent meaning structures (LMS) and for understanding how LMS sustain and permeate people's biographies;
- This three-level social ontology is related to RBR approach in order to differentiate experienced life history, narrated life story and LMS as distinct ontological and analytical levels;
- By adopting the CR's principles of emergence and non-reduction, RBR researchers are protected from the risk to consider the above-mentioned

levels (experienced life-history and narrated life-story) as being connected and related to each other in a one-way and mechanistic way.
Rather, the multiple mediations between experienced life history and
narrated life-story are brought to the fore: through the narrator's present
perspective about past experiences, the role of memory, the context of
the interview situation and through the impact of dominant discourses
and counter-discourses;

- Both CR and RBR make sense of lived experience and biographical
  constructions not as a personal "achievement" but as relationally constituted, shaped in conjunction with relational goods or relational evils
  as well as with power asymmetries;
- Both CR and RBR prioritize the processual grounding of social phenomena through the concept of sequentiality. Assessing biographical
  experiences is related to how the "then" and the "now" are inscribed
  either in the life history or in the life story, respectively;
- Finally, both CR and RBR put at the centre of their attention the morphogenetic and morphostatic processes of the social phenomena.

What these points seek to underline is the theoretical and methodological
advantages both CR and RBR share and the gains obtained should these
points be "translated" into research practice. In particular, the gains RBR
obtains through the use of CR as a philosophical ground have to do with the
fact that biographical research overcomes the impasses and shortcomings
of radical constructivist trends, which propound the idea that biographical research's sole goal should be the study of free-floating narratives and
of their functions in interview situations. Researchers, these trends hold,
should limit themselves to exploring how narrations are constructed, leav-
ing aside "why" questions. However, as we showed in chapter 7, such a perspective reduces the object of study of biographical research to a discursive
artefact and to a performative achievement of interlocutors and it is incapable of theorizing a biography as a socio-historical construct whose causes
are tied up with specific relational mechanisms. By putting at the forefront
of its philosophical thinking the causal explanation of social phenomena,
CR underscores the necessity of tracing the generative mechanisms of
social events and of how they are experienced by the acting subjects. In
this way, the historical and relational conditions of meaning-making processes brought to light and the traps of "hermeneutic idealism" are avoided
(Habermas 1981, 223).

On the other hand, by using the toolbox of RBR, CR enables researchers to highlight in an empirical way the causal conditions that make
things happen and the causal chains through which social phenomena are

produced (see also Gross 2018). Given that RBR acknowledges the historicity of lived experiences, researchers may explore one of the main theoretical ideas of CR, namely the temporal and contextual grounding of self-formation and of the decision-making process. Furthermore, we have put forward an emergentist theory of social action in which reasons for action are not phantasms of discourses, as radical constructivists hold, but rather the real causes of action. This does not mean that action is explained by them, but that one has to reformulate how people make decisions (Elder-Vass 2007). This reformulation fits perfectly with RBR's perspective that habitus and reflexivity coexist. Decisions and reasons are "intakes" that affect in various degrees the shaping of an action. Thus, reasons which are held in varying degrees of commitment predispose agents to behave in a given way in the future in certain circumstances. Reasons and actions cannot be seen as empirical regularities because the former are contingent on the operation of other causal powers with the capacity to co-determine our decisions and our subsequent behaviour. Consequently, some aspects of our behaviour may be attributed to dispositions or habitus and others to conscious reflection. It is exactly this interplay between habitus and reflexivity that RBR tries to analyze by exploring how the emergent properties of the relations in which people live throughout their lives give shape to these two aspects. However, we believe that the range and the details of this interplay are a matter of social research, rather than a problem that can be solved through theoretical reflections alone. In this sense, it is research practice that will evaluate the benefits obtained by the philosophical, theoretical and methodological arguments we have tried to present in this book.

References

Bunge, M. *Causality and Modern Science*. New York: Dover Publications, 2009.

Donati, P. "Social Mechanisms and Their Feedbacks: Mechanical vs Relational Emergence of New Social Formations." In *Generative Mechanisms Transforming the Social Order*, edited by M. Archer, 65–95. New York: Springer, 2015.

Elder-Vass, D. "Reconciling Archer and Bourdieu in an Emergentist Theory of Action." *Sociological Theory* 25, no. 4 (2007): 325–45. doi:10.1111/j.1467-9558.2007.00312.x.

Gross, N. "The Structure of Causal Chains." *Sociological Theory* 36, no. 4 (2018): 1–25. doi:10.1177/0735275118811377.

Habermas, J. 1981. *Theorie des kommunikativen Handelns*. Zweiter Band. Frankfurt/M: Suhrkamp.

Kim, J. "Making Sense of Emergence." *Philosophical Studies* 95, no. 1/2 (1999): 3–36.

Sawyer, R.K. "The Mechanisms of Emergence." *Philosophy of the Social Sciences* 34, no. 2 (2004): 260–85. doi:10.1177/0048393103262553.

Sawyer, R.K. *Social Emergence. Societies as Complex Systems*. Cambridge: Cambridge University Press, 2005.

Steel, D. "Causal Inference and Social Mechanisms." *Philosophy of the Social Sciences* 34, no. 1 (2004): 55–78. doi:10.1177/0048393103260775.

Index

For Product Safety Concerns and Information please contact our EU
representative GPSR@taylorandfrancis.com
Taylor & Francis Verlag GmbH, Kaufingerstraße 24, 80331 München, Germany